One Hundred Red Hot Years

Big Moments of the 20th Century

a book in the Radical History series

radical historY

radical historY █

Also published in the Radical History series:

Politics on Trial: *Five Famous Trials of the 20th Century*

Chile: *the Other September 11*

IWW: *A Wobbly Vision of the World*

The massive anticapitalist protest movements storming our globe prove that people have not surrendered to the lie of the "end of history" or submitted to the ever-deadening, ever-demoralizing capitalist status quo.

Radical History, an exciting new series from Ocean Press, challenges the attempt to separate human beings from their histories and communities and reflects a confidence in humanity's capacity to change our society and ourselves.

Radical History seeks to revive events, struggles and people erased from conventional (and conservative) media and memory, providing invaluable resources for a new generation of political activists.

The series will include eyewitness accounts and historic, forgotten or ignored documents. It will publish speeches and articles as well as new essays, chronologies and further resources. These books are edited and designed by young political activists.

Series Editor: Deborah Shnookal

"What history really shows is that today's empire is tomorrow's ashes."

–Mumia Abu-Jamal

One Hundred Red Hot Years

Big Moments of the 20th Century

Preface by Eduardo Galeano

Edited by Deborah Shnookal

Ocean Press
Melbourne ■ New York
www.oceanbooks.com.au

Cover photo: Nicaragua, 1983.

Cover design by Meaghan Barbuto

Copyright © 2003 Ocean Press

All rights reserved. No part of this publication may be reproduced, stored in a retrieval system or transmitted in any form or by any means, electronic, mechanical, photocopying, recording or otherwise, without the prior permission of the publisher.

ISBN 1-876175-48-6

First printed 2003

Printed in Australia

Library of Congress Control Number 2002107122

Published by Ocean Press

Australia GPO Box 3279 Melbourne, Victoria 3001, Australia
Tel 61 3 9326 4280
Fax 61 3 9329 5040
email: info@oceanbooks.com.au

USA PO Box 1186 Old Chelsea Station, New York, NY 10113-1186, USA
Tel 718 246 4160

Ocean Press Distributors

United States and Canada

Consortium Sales & Book Distribution
1045 Westgate Drive, Suite 90
Saint Paul, MN 55114-1065
1 800 283 3572

Britain and Europe

Global Book Marketing
38 King Street, London WC2E 8JT, UK
orders@globalbookmarketing.co.uk

Australia and New Zealand

Astam Books
57-61 John Street, Leichhardt, NSW 2040, Australia
info@astambooks.com.au

Cuba and Latin America

Ocean Press
Calle 21 #406, Vedado, Havana, Cuba

www.oceanbooks.com.au

CONTENTS

"As long as someone controls your history, the truth shall remain just a mystery."

–Ben Harper

EDITOR'S NOTE

WITH GREAT GLEE AND GLOATING, the "end of history" was proclaimed even before the close of the millennium. The "destruction of the past, or rather the social mechanisms that link one's contemporary experience to that of earlier generations, is one of the most characteristic and eerie phenomena of the late 20th century," writes historian Eric Hobsbawm. The result, he says, is that most of us now "grow up in a sort of permanent present." The study of history has been downgraded or "downsized" in our schools and colleges. Why bother with the past if there can be no future but the present?

The problem: without a consciousness of what has gone before, it is difficult to imagine a different future.

This modest volume in no way presumes to offer a history of the last century. It is not intended as a nostalgic journey or as a guidebook for future struggles. But by providing a fleeting glimpse of the great triumphs and turbulence over 100 years of revolution, reaction and resistance, this book and others published in our "Radical History" and "Rebel Lives" series suggest that humanity has not always accepted the global ravages of capitalism and that we have constantly strived to reclaim the future — in the belief that we can reshape both our society and ourselves.

As Bernadette Devlin once said, "We were born into an unjust system. We are not prepared to grow old in it."

With similar confidence, one of *Time* magazine's iconic figures of the century, Che Guevara, challenged skeptics: "And if someone says we are just romantics, inveterate idealists, thinking the impossible, that the masses of people cannot be transformed into almost archetypical human beings, we will have to answer a thousand and one times: Yes, it can be done. We know we are right — humanity can advance."

Will we succeed? Commenting on the incredibly audacious uprising of 1871 when the people of Paris set up their own government or commune, Karl Marx wrote: "World history would indeed be very easy to make if the struggle were taken up only on condition of infallibly favorable chances…" Unsure of whether or not the Paris Commune would survive, he nevertheless urged international solidarity arguing that it represented a new phase in "the struggle of the working class against the capitalist class and its state."

In his preface to this book, Eduardo Galeano readily acknowledges that "history makes mistakes, that it gets distracted, falls asleep, loses its way. We make it, and it looks like us. But, like us, it is also unpredictable… Against all forecasts, against all evidence, the little guy sometimes leads the invincible giant a merry dance."

As the new century begins, from Porto Alegre to Genoa to Seattle, the "invincible giant" has again been led on a "merry dance." So let's dance!

Deborah Shnookal

poster © OSPAAAL (Organization in Solidarity with the
Peoples of Africa, Asia and Latin America)

P R E F A C E

BETRAYAL AND PROMISE

Eduardo Galeano

THE 20TH CENTURY WAS BORN under the sign of revolution, and it dies marked by despair. Stop the world, I want to get off: in these times of stupor and collapse, the ranks of the regretful are swelling — regretful of political passion and regretful of all passion. There are many who apologize for having believed that it was possible to conquer heaven; there are many who fervently seek to kick over their own traces and climb down from hope, as if hope were a worn-out horse.

End of the century, end of the millennium: end of the world? How much unpoisoned air have we still got left? How many unspoiled lands, how many waters not yet dead? How many non-ailing souls? In its Hebrew version, the word sick means "without a project," and this is the gravest sickness among the many plagues of our times. But someone, who knows who, wrote in passing on a wall in the city of Bogotá: "Let's leave pessimism for better times."

Whenever we take it into our heads to express hope in

Spanish, we say: *abrigamos esperanzas* ("we shelter hope"). Nice expression, nice challenge: sheltering it to prevent it from dying of cold in the implacably rough climate of our present times. According to a recent survey carried out in 17 Latin American countries, three out of four people describe their situation as stagnant or worsening. Is it necessary to accept misfortune as one accepts winter or death? It is time for we Latin Americans to start asking: are we going to resign ourselves to enduring life and to being no more than a caricature of the North? No more than a mirror which multiplies the distortions of the original image? The look-after-number-one attitude degenerating into "let them die if they can't"? Swarms of losers in a race where the majority are pushed off the track? Crime turned to slaughter, urban hysteria elevated to total madness? Have we nothing else to say and to live through?

Fortunately, we hardly ever hear history described as infallible these days. We are well aware by now that history makes mistakes, that it gets distracted, falls asleep, loses its way. We make it, and it looks like us. But, like us, it is also unpredictable. It is with human history as with football: its best feature is its ability to surprise. Against all forecasts, against all evidence, the little guy sometimes leads the invincible giant on a merry dance.

However messed-up the warp of reality, new fabrics are being woven on to it, and those fabrics are made up of a weft of many and diverse colors. Alternative social movements express themselves not only through parties and unions, but in other ways too. There is nothing spectacular about the process, and it happens mostly at a local level, but everywhere, on a worldwide scale, a thousand and one new forces are emerging. They sprout from the bottom up and from inside outwards. Without any fuss, they put their shoulder to the wheel of rebuilding democracy, nourished by popular participation, and are reclaiming the battered traditions of tolerance, mutual help and communion with nature. One of their spokespeople, Manfred Max-Neef, defines them as a cloud of mosquitoes launched against a system which spurns embraces and forces us to jostle. "The mosquito cloud," he says, "is more powerful than the rhinoceros. It grows and grows, buzzes and buzzes."

In Latin America, they are a dangerous and expanding species: the organizations of the landless, the homeless, the jobless, all the lesses; the groups working for human rights; the white scarves of the mothers and grandmothers who oppose the impunity of power; the neighborhood movements; the citizens' groups fighting for fair prices and healthy products; those who struggle against racial and sexual discrimination, against machismo and against the exploitation of children; the ecologists; the pacifists; the health workers and popular educators; those who trigger collective creation and those who rescue collective memory; the cooperatives engaged in organic agriculture; community radio and television stations; and many other voices of popular participation which are neither the spare tires of any party nor chapels subject to any Vatican. These driving forces of civil society are frequently persecuted by the powers-that-be, sometimes by means of the bullet. Some activists fall, riddled with bullets, on the way. May the gods and the devils rest their souls: it's the fruit-yielding trees that the stones are thrown at.

With one or two exceptions, like the Zapatistas of Chiapas and the landless in Brazil, it is rare for these movements to be at the forefront of public attention; and not just because they don't deserve it. Just to mention one case, one of these popular organizations, born in recent years and unknown outside the borders of its own country, has set an example which the Latin American presidents ought to follow. El Barzón is the name of an organization of debtors who have joined together in Mexico to defend themselves against the usury of the banks. El Barzón sprang up spontaneously. Initially, they were few. Few, but contagious. Now they are a multitude.

Our presidents would do well to learn from that experience, enabling countries to unite, as people did in Mexico, and form a single front against the financial despotism which imposes its will by negotiating with each country separately. But the presidents' ears are full of the resonant platitudes they exchange each time they meet and pose for the family photograph, with the president of the United States — the Mother Country — always in the center.

It's happening in many places on the Latin American map: people are uniting against the paralyzing gases of fear and, united, they are learning not to bow their heads. As Old Antonio says: "Everyone is as small as the fear they feel, and as big as the enemy they choose." No longer cowed, these people are saying their piece. To give another Mexican example, the Zapatistas' Subcomandante Marcos speaks for the unders: the underdeveloped, the underfed, the undermined, the underheard. The indigenous communities of Chiapas discuss and decide, and he is their mouthpiece. The voice of those who have no voice? They, who have been forced into silence, are the voice. They speak through what they say and they speak through their silence.

The official history, a mutilated memory, is a long ceremony of self-praise by those who call the shots in this world. Their reflectors, which illuminate the peaks, leave the base in the dark. The usual invisible beings form part, at best, of the scenery of history, like Hollywood extras. But it is they, the actors in the real history, the denied, lied-about, hidden protagonists of past and present reality, who embody the splendid fan of another possible reality. Blinded by elitism, racism, sexism and militarism, the United States continues to ignore the plenitude within it. And this is doubly true in the South: Latin America is endowed with the most fabulous human and vegetal diversity on the planet. This is where its fecundity and promise reside. As the anthropologist Rodolfo Stavenhagen puts it: "Cultural diversity is to the human species what biological diversity is to the world's genetic wealth." To enable these energies to express the possible wonders of the people and the land, one would have to start by not confusing identity with archaeology, or nature with scenery. Identity is not something frozen in the museums, nor is ecology reducible to gardening.

Five centuries ago, the people and the lands of the Americas were incorporated into the world market as things. A few conquerors, the conquered conquerors, were able to fathom the American plurality, and they lived within it and for it; but the Conquest, a blind and blinding enterprise like all imperial invasions, was capable of recognizing the indigenous people, and nature, only as objects to be exploited or as obstacles. Cultural diversity was dismissed as ignorance and punished as heresy, in the name of a single god, a single language and a single truth, and this sin of idolatry merited flogging, hanging or the stake.

There is no longer talk of subjecting nature: now its executioners prefer to say that it has to be protected. But in either case, then and now, nature is external to us: the civilization that confuses clocks with the time also confuses nature with postcards. But the vitality of the world, which mocks all classifications and is beyond all explanations, never stays still. Nature realizes itself in movement, as do we, its children, who are what we are at the same time as we are what we do to change what we are. As Paolo Freire, the educator who died learning, said: "We exist in motion."

The truth is in the journey, not in the port. There is no truth but the quest for truth. Are we condemned to criminality? We are well aware of the fact that we human creatures are very busy devouring our fellow human beings and devastating the planet, but we also know that we wouldn't be here if our remote Paleolithic ancestors had been unable to adapt to the nature they were part of, or had not been willing to share what they hunted and gathered. No matter where, how or when a person may live, each one contains within themselves many possible persons, and it's the ruling system, which has nothing eternal about it, that invites our basest occupants on to the stage every day, while preventing the others from growing and banning them from making an appearance. We may be badly made, but we're not finished yet; and it's the adventure of making changes and changing ourselves which makes worthwhile this flicker in the history of the universe that we are, this fleeting warmth between two glaciers.

OSPAAAL

jornada de solidaridad con puerto rico / sept 23 journée de
solidarité avec porto rico / sept 23   day of solidarity with
puerto rico / sept 23 يومية التضامن مع شعب بورتوريكو ٢٣ ايلول

poster © OSPAAAL

ONE

U.S. AGGRESSION

AGAINST LATIN AMERICA

Luis Suárez

> "The United States seems destined to plague and torment the [Latin American] continent in the name of freedom."
> –Simon Bolívar

1900 After its military occupation of the island in 1898, the U.S. Government imposes the Foraker Act on the people of Puerto Rico, officially turning the nation into a U.S. colony.

1902 Washington imposes the infamous Platt Amendment on the Republic of Cuba as a condition for withdrawal of U.S. military forces that had occupied the island since the so-called Spanish American War (1898). As a result, Cuba becomes a virtual U.S. protectorate. The amendment also appropriates part of Guantánamo Bay, where a U.S. naval base is established.

1903 U.S. Marines land in Honduras and later the Dominican Republic under the pretext of "protecting U.S. interests." During the same year, U.S. forces occupy Panama and bring about its separation from the Republic of Colombia. The United States later "negotiates" a treaty with the newly formed pseudo-Republic of Panama, thereby assuming control of the Panama Canal Zone.

1905 Under the guise of the Roosevelt Corollary, U.S. troops occupy the Dominican Republic, taking control of its customs authority to guarantee payment of the debts the Dominican Government has with several European and U.S. creditors.

1906 U.S. armed forces once again occupy Cuba at the request of its puppet, President Tomás Estrada Palma. The country remains under occupation until 1909.

1907 With the outbreak of fighting between Honduras and Nicaragua, U.S. Marines occupy the cities of Trujillo, Cieba, Puerto Cortés, San Pedro and Choloma, protecting U.S. interests in both countries.

1909 U.S. Marines occupy Nicaragua and remain there until 1925.

1912 U.S. troops intervene in Panama to run the presidential elections there; in Cuba to support the bloody repression of an uprising by the Independent Movement of People of Color; and, again, in Puerto Cortés, Honduras.

1914 U.S. Marines loot the National Bank of Port au Prince, Haiti; land in the Dominican Republic; and occupy the city of Veracruz, Mexico, to support reactionary forces that oppose the popular and anti-imperialist principles of the 1910 Mexican Revolution.

1915 U.S. troops occupy Haiti to prevent Rosalvo Bobo, known for his anti-U.S. positions, from becoming president. This occupation lasts until August 1934, using brutal measures to defeat the armed resistance of the Haitian people. The resistance is organized by the *cacós* and led by Charlemagne Peralte, until his murder by a U.S. Marine officer.

1916 There is another landing in the Dominican Republic. Popular resistance by the *gavilleros* is drowned in blood and firepower. The country remains under military occupation until 1925. U.S. Marines train the police forces that bring Rafael Leonidas Trujillo to power in 1930.

1917 A contingent of U.S. Marines lands in Cuba to strengthen the pro-imperialist government of conservative President Mario García Menocal. Menocal faces the Liberal Party *Chambelona* insurrection. Also in the same year, 10,000 U.S. soldiers, led by General Pushing, invade Mexican territory in a "punitive" intervention to put down the popular forces headed by Pancho Villa.

1918-20 U.S. troops land and intervene in Panama, Honduras and Guatemala.

1924-25 U.S. troops intervene in the Honduran civil war, which has been provoked by the U.S.-owned United Fruit and Coyumel companies. During the same period, U.S. adventurer Richard O. March, former chargé d'affaires in Panama, tries to divide Panama by creating the "Republic of Tule." The author of this frustrated attempt is rescued and sent to the United States aboard a U.S. warship.

1926 U.S. Marines land in Nicaragua to put down a liberal rebellion against the pro-U.S. government of Adolfo Díaz. Augustino César Sandino heads the victorious resistance against this latest military invasion. Despite brutal measures of repression against the Nicaraguan people and faced with an inability to put down Sandino's "Crazy Little Army," at the end of 1932 the United States trains a National Guard, headed by Anastasio Somoza García.

"Somoza may be a son of a bitch, but he's our son of a bitch."

–Franklin D. Roosevelt commenting on Nicaraguan dictator Anastasio Somoza

1932 U.S. warships enter the Salvadoran port city of Acajutla to "prevent disorder that would affect U.S. interests." Thus protected, dictator Maximiliano Hernández murders 30,000 Salvadorans with impunity in order to crush a popular insurrection headed by Farabundo Martí.

1933 Despite the "good neighbor policy" announced by Franklin Delano Roosevelt (1933-45), General Somoza orders the murder — under instructions from the U.S. ambassador in Managua — of Augustino César Sandino, "the general of free men." The long-lasting Somoza dynasty is installed under U.S. protection. During the same year, the United States establishes a blockade of Cuba and threatens intervention to check a popular uprising that overthrew bloodthirsty dictator Gerardo Machado and replaced him with a provisional government headed by Dr. Ramón Grau San Martín.

1934 Through various diplomatic maneuvers, the United States carries out a new show of force around the island of Cuba to support the coup d'état led by Sergeant Fulgencio Batista that overthrows the provisional government of Dr. Ramón Grau San Martín. With the backing of the U.S. ambassador in Havana, Batista orders the execution of popular leader Antonio Guiteras and the bloody repression of a general strike against the newly installed puppet government.

1935 U.S. troops, who since the dawn of the century had occupied Puerto Rico, violently repress the independence struggles of the Borinquen people. There is a massacre in Rio Piedras.

1937 In the city of Ponce, U.S. occupation forces crush massive, popular demonstrations calling for Puerto Rican independence from U.S. colonial rule.

1938 U.S. and British monopolies, with the complicity of Washington, undertake an economic embargo of Mexico, following a decision by the sovereign government of Lázaro Cárdenas to nationalize the nation's oil resources. The U.S. embassy in Mexico City is implicated in various conspiracies, including a frustrated military uprising aimed at destabilizing and ultimately overthrowing the popular, nationalist government.

1944 U.S. naval units occupy the port of Buenos Aires to force the government to break diplomatic relations with and declare war on the Nazi-fascist Axis powers of Germany, Italy and Japan. Colonel Juan Domingo Perón plays a prominent role in this government, which took office following a military revolution in 1943.

1947 Under pressure from the United States, all Latin American governments sign the ill-named Inter-American Treaty of Reciprocal Assistance. This treaty becomes a model for all the political-military pacts — North Atlantic Treaty Organization (NATO), Southeast Asia Treaty Organization (SEATO) and Central Treaty Organization (CENTO) — pursued by Washington as part of its "strategy of communist containment."

1948 The Organization of American States (OAS) is institutionalized. It is stained in blood shed by the Colombian people during the disorganized *Bogotazo* popular insurrection, the draconian repression that followed the assassination of popular leader Jorge Eliecer Gaitán, and formed under pressure from the United States.

1950 U.S. armed forces strangle the October 30 uprising for Puerto Rican independence. The United States also facilitated the installation of the ill-named Associated Free State in July 1952, which has served ever since as a façade for iron-fisted colonial domination of this Caribbean island.

1954 In Operation Success, shamefully backed by the OAS, the United States stages a mercenary invasion against the popular, nationalist government of Jacobo Arbenz in Guatemala. It has the direct support of U.S. planes based in the Panama Canal Zone and the further support of the military dictatorships of El Salvador, Honduras and Nicaragua. Following Arbenz's resignation, a puppet government under Colonel Carlos Castillo Armas is installed, which initiates a campaign of bloody repression against the Guatemalan people.

1955 With direct support from the U.S. ambassador in Buenos Aires, the constitutional government of Juan Domingo Perón is overthrown in a bloody coup d'état. U.S. Marines and the British Navy supply the Argentine Navy with the munitions used to bomb the government palace and the Plaza de Mayo.

1958 The dictatorship of Fulgencio Batista, with Pentagon backing, undertakes a massive military operation designed to defeat the Rebel Army. After the failure of that offensive, Washington and the U.S. embassy in Havana carry out various operations, including a call for elections and an attempted coup d'état, to thwart the victory of the Cuban Revolution. On January 1, 1959, a revolutionary general strike, called by Fidel Castro's July 26 Movement, defeats Washington's plot.

1961 The U.S. Government finances and organizes the invasion at the Bay of Pigs in Cuba. This attempt to destroy the Cuban Revolution collapses in 72 hours. Many months of criminal aggressions against Cuba and support for counterrevolutionary violence on the island follow. Washington spearheads diplomatic actions that result in the expulsion of Cuba from the OAS.

1962 President Kennedy authorizes a military blockade of Cuba, aimed at preventing the Cuban people and government from housing weapons from the Soviet Union necessary to defend their national sovereignty. The conflict brings the world to the brink of nuclear war in October as part of what becomes known as the Cuban Missile Crisis.

1964 The popular government of the People's Progressive Party of Guyana, led by Prime Minister Cheddi Jagan, is overthrown following various economic and political maneuvers aided and abetted by Washington and the CIA. During the same year, U.S. armed forces violently repress a student demonstration demanding Panamanian sovereignty over the Canal Zone. Likewise, the Colombian Government, with Pentagon backing, concludes the Latin American Security Operation, aimed at putting down with firepower the ill-named "independent republics" of Marquetalia, Rio Chiquito, El Pato and Guayabero, where, since the end of the 1950s, the Colombian Communist Party has had strong political influence.

1965 42,000 U.S. troops, supported by the OAS, intervene in the Dominican Republic to overthrow the popular and constitutional revolution headed by Colonel Francisco Caamaño Deñó. The occupation produces a puppet government that continues repression against the constitutional forces.

1967 Following orders from Washington, Ernesto Che Guevara and others among his guerrilla group are murdered in Bolivia. The crime involved the notable participation of CIA agents.

1970 In close coordination and support from the CIA station in Santiago de Chile, General Rene Schneider, head of the Chilean Army, is assassinated in an attempt to prevent the Chilean Congress from ratifying the electoral victory of Popular Unity leader Salvador Allende. In that same year, the Túpac Amaru Liberation Movement condemns the U.S. embassy in Montevideo and CIA advisers — including the infamous Dan Mitrione — for participating in repression against the revolutionary movements in Uruguay.

1972 U.S. foreign policy and security establishment is openly implicated in the bloody defeat of a popular uprising that breaks out in

El Salvador. The uprising is in reaction to electoral fraud led by Colonel Armando Molina, front man for the Salvadoran oligarchy. Military action is supported by the Central American Defense Council (Honduras, Guatemala, El Salvador and Nicaragua), headed by the Pentagon.

1973 With involvement by Washington and the CIA, the constitutional president of Chile, Salvador Allende, is assassinated on September 11 in a coup d'état. This begins the lengthy military dictatorship of General Augusto Pinochet (1973-90). During the same year, backed by the United States, a fascist-like military dictatorship is institutionalized in Uruguay.

"I don't see why we need to stand by and watch a country go communist because of the irresponsibility of its own people."

–Henry Kissinger on the prospect of Allende's election victory in Chile in 1970

1979 With logistical support provided by Washington, the Pentagon and the U.S. Southern Command (operating from the Panama Canal Zone), Anastasio Somoza's dictatorship in Nicaragua savagely represses a popular uprising led by the Sandinista National Liberation Front (FSLN). Despite this and extensive U.S. economic and military aid to Somoza, the Sandinista Revolution triumphs on July 19.

1980 Organized by the United States and generously financed by Washington, Nicaraguan counterrevolutionary forces begin to operate from bases in Honduras. Close to 30,000 Nicaraguans are killed during the near decade-long "dirty war" carried out against the people of Nicaragua by the administrations of Ronald Reagan and George Bush.

1982 Washington and the Chilean military dictatorship back the military actions of the Thatcher Government in its attempt to maintain British colonial rule over Argentina's Malvinas Islands.

1983 Following the shadowy murder of Prime Minister Maurice Bishop and others involved in the Grenadan Revolution, U.S. armed forces invade the small island of Grenada. That same year, under the so-called Caribbean Initiative, the White House and the

Pentagon carry out an intense militarization of the Caribbean Basin, particularly the Central American countries. This results in the strengthening and prolonging of the military dictatorships in El Salvador and Guatemala, directly responsible for close to 300,000 murders in both countries.

1989 Following various efforts to destabilize civil and military authorities in Panama both politically and economically, U.S. troops invade and occupy the isthmus, killing thousands of civilians and installing the puppet government of Guillermo Endara.

1992 As part of its prolonged economic and political warfare against the Cuban Revolution, Washington passes the Torricelli amendment, tightening the blockade.

1994 In the name of democracy and free market expansion announced by the administration of Bill Clinton (1993-2000), U.S. troops (with the backing of the UN Security Council) intervene militarily in Haiti. Aside from its proclaimed goals, the United States continues to guarantee impunity for crimes committed by subsequent military governments following the bloody coup d'état of 1990 that overthrew the constitutionally elected president, Jean Bertrand Aristide.

1996 President Clinton announces the Helms-Burton Law, instigated by reactionary elements in Congress and Cuban American terrorist groups operating in Miami. This law attempts to extend the extra-territorial reach of the U.S. blockade of Cuba and push non-U.S. companies and countries to break ties with Cuba.

2000 Backed by Congress, President Clinton approves Plan Colombia. Under the guise of combating the drug trade, it is aimed at destroying the resources and, above all, the base of support for the Colombian guerrillas.

From Luis Suárez Salazar, Terror and Violence in Latin America, *to be published in 2003 by Ocean Press. A version of this chronology appeared in the magazine* Tricontinental *in 2001.*

One Big Union Monthly, IWW poster, 1920

T W O

ONE HUNDRED RED HOT YEARS

1898 **World** United States seizes Philippines, Cuba, Puerto Rico and Guam from Spain.

1899 **World** U. S. troops sent to Nicaragua, Samoa and against miners in Idaho.

1900 **World** The first Pan-African Congress is held in London but with no delegates from Africa itself, only from the black diaspora. The Socialist International's fifth congress pledges to organize against militarism.

China The Boxer Rebellion, a violent uprising against the cultural and political influence of the Western powers, culminates in a 56-day siege of the foreign enclaves in Beijing. It is eventually ruthlessly put down by Western troops.

South Africa The Boer War continues as Britain annexes the Boer republics of Orange Free State and Transvaal.

West Africa Thousands of Asante rebels attack Britain's Kumasi fort in Gold Coast.

Philippines Rebels who began their liberation struggle against the Spanish now fight U.S. rule.
East Indies Tjoakraminoto leads the challenge to Dutch colonial domination.
Burma U Ba Pe leads increasing resistance to British control.
United States Socialist Eugene V. Debs runs for president.

1901

Russia Students in St. Petersburg set up barricades and call for the Czar's overthrow; they are joined by the writer Leo Tolstoy.
West Africa Britain annexes the Asante Kingdom as part of Gold Coast.
United States Army sent to quash Oklahoma Indian revolt.

1902

South Africa The Vereeniging Treaty ends the Boer War; Boers must accept British rule but are promised self-government later.
Russia The head of the secret police is killed by socialists. Thousands die in workers' riots; the Czar offers talks.

1903

Congo Human rights campaign against 20-year Belgian genocide.
Central America The United States backs a rebellion in Panama to throw out Colombians opposed to the Panama Canal.
Russia The Social Democrats split into Bolsheviks ("majority") and Mensheviks ("minority").
Nigeria The British-led West African Frontier Force takes Kano and Sokoto; the sultan flees.
Korea Japanese Marines suppress rioting workers.
Britain Emmeline Pankhurst founds the militant Women's Suffrage and Political Union in Manchester.
United States Mother Jones leads child workers in demanding a 55-hour week.

1904

Korea U. S. Marines land during Russo-Japanese war (1904-05).
East Indies The Dutch kill 541 Acehnese people in a revolt on Sumatra.
Tibet Invading British forces kill 500 Tibetans; they reach Lhasa and the Dalai Lama flees. The British withdraw after Tibet agrees not to cede territory to any other foreign power.

1905

Russia The Czar's troops shoot 500 demonstrators dead on Bloody Sunday; sailors mutiny on the battleship *Potemkin*; there is a general strike in St. Petersburg; the uprising is crushed after a week of street fighting.

United States The Industrial Workers of the World (IWW) is founded at a conference in Chicago, attended by "Big Bill" Haywood and Mother Jones. The "Wobblies" seek to organize workers in one big union, undivided by craft, sex or race, and become target of government repression.

Southwest Africa An insurrection by the Herero people is followed by a German revenge campaign driving 5,000 into the desert to die of thirst; three in four Hereros die.

British East Africa The Nandi resistance leader Koitalel is assassinated by a British officer.

Britain Christabel Pankhurst and Annie Kenney become the first two suffragettes to go to prison, sentenced for assaulting police.

1906

Nigeria British troops quell protests by Tiv people against Muslim Hausa rule.

South Africa British troops kill 60 Zulus protesting the poll tax.

Guatemala is defeated after invading both Honduras and El Salvador.

India The Indian National Congress adopts the idea of *swaraj* or "self-rule" for the first time.

1907

German East Africa The great rebel leader Abdallah Mapanda, coordinator of the Maji-Maji uprisings over the last 18 months, is captured.

Honduras U.S. Marines land on March 21.

Congo King Leopold sells his personal fiefdom to the Belgian state.

1908

Turkey Uprising by the Young Turks forces the sultan to restore the constitution, which has been suspended for 32 years.

1909

Persia British troops land as fear of famine causes unrest. The shah breaks a promise of elections. Nationalists seize Tehran, imposing a new shah.

Spain An antigovernment revolt in Catalonia leaves 1,000 dead. Anarchist Francisco Ferrer is shot by firing squad.

Egypt A youth congress demands the British withdraw.

United States 97 African Americans lynched.

1910

Africa Belgium, Britain and Germany fix the borders of Congo, Uganda and German East Africa.

Tibet The Dalai Lama flees to India as Chinese troops invade Lhasa, only two months after his return from exile in Beijing.

Germany Socialists are shot and sabred in a suffrage demonstration in Berlin.

Portugal After a republican coup the monarchy and the nobility are abolished.

Korea is annexed by Japan.

Mexico Revolution stirs as the country's dictator for almost 45 years, Porfirio Díaz, is challenged by liberal reformer Francisco Madero and guerrilla leaders Pancho Villa and Emiliano Zapata.

"Better to die on your feet than live on your knees."
–Emiliano Zapata

1911

Britain Home Secretary Winston Churchill refuses to allow in the fire brigade to stop three anarchists burning to death while under siege from 1,000 troops and police.

United States Triangle Shirtwaist factory fire kills 146 on March 25; exit doors were locked. Triangle owners subsequently indicted for manslaughter.

Mexico U.S. troops cross the Rio Grande and fight the rebels under Madero, who refuses a ceasefire; crowds take to the streets to support the rebels; Díaz resigns and Madero becomes president.

Morocco Rebellion breaks out and France sends troops to occupy Fez; Germany agrees to French control in return for dominion over a million people formerly under French rule in Central Africa.

China Republican revolution sweeps the country. Sun Yatsen becomes leader of a provisional republican government.

1912
Britain Suffragettes smash shop windows throughout London's West End and hurl stones at 10 Downing Street; suffragettes on hunger strike are force-fed in prison.
Honduras In February U.S. Marines land.
Cuba U.S. Marines land in June.
Nicaragua In August U.S. Marines land.
India A bomb wounds the British Governor General as he rides an elephant to celebrate the opening of the new capital in Delhi.
South Africa The African National Congress (ANC) is formed to fight racial discrimination.

1913
Britain Suffragette leader Emmeline Pankhurst is given three years in prison for blowing up Lloyd George's new golf villa. Emily Davison tries to stop the king's horse at the Derby and dies from her injuries; thousands watch her funeral procession. Suffragettes bomb ministers' country homes.
United States Thousands march on Washington on March 3 demanding women's suffrage.
Mexico President Madero is deposed, arrested and shot dead. Congress is dissolved; Pancho Villa rebels again and captures Ciudad Juárez.
Europe German and French socialists produce an antiwar manifesto.
United States IWW-led Paterson Silk strikers starved into defeat.
Belgium Coalminers prompt a general strike.
World International Women's Peace Conference held in The Hague.
South Africa A peaceful march of 2,500 Indians in Transvaal protests a new law requiring Indians not to move from their registered province. Its leader, Mohandas Gandhi, is sentenced to nine months in jail.

1914
South Africa A general strike results in martial law and the secret deportation of 10 strike leaders.
Mexico 3,000 U.S. Marines seize the port of Vera Cruz. A peace

agreement leaves the United States in control of the city as the dictator Huerta resigns.

United States Massacre of striking coalminers, wives and children in Ludlow, Colorado, on April 20.

World Austria declares war on Serbia and invades after Archduke Ferdinand is assassinated. Russia mobilizes in support of Serbia and Germany declares war on Russia and France. Britain declares war when Germany invades Belgium. Japan declares war on Germany. Britain's colonies join the war: New Zealand forces occupy German-controlled Samoa; Australians invade German New Guinea; South African troops attack German Southwest Africa; and Indian troops are sent to fight in German East Africa.

United States Western Federation of Miners strikers crushed by militia in Butte on November 13.

1915

United States Supreme Court upholds "yellow dog" contracts, which forbid membership in labor unions.

Britain The Trades Union Congress opposes conscription. Radical papers are closed down, including the socialist *Labour Leader, Forward,* and the anticonscription *Tribunal.*

United States The IWW's Joe Hill is shot by firing squad in Utah on November 19. His last words are "Don't waste time in mourning. Organize!"

1916

Ireland Republicans revolt at Easter against British rule capturing part of Dublin. They are defeated and seven rebel leaders are executed, including James Connolly.

Mexico Rebel leader Pancho Villa leads a raid into the United States, killing 17. He is pursued back into Mexico by 6,000 U.S. soldiers and captured.

Middle East Britain and France agree to carve up the former Turkish empire between them after the war, with Britain to run Palestine and Mesopotamia and France to get Syria.

World Socialist pacifists attend an International Socialist Conference in Kienthal, Switzerland.

Germany Socialist Karl Liebknecht leads peace demonstrations which spread to 35 cities. Liebknecht is sentenced to four years in prison.

United States Railroad workers win 8-hour day on September 3.

Suffragette poster, 1906

United States Massacre of Wobbly strikers at Everett, Washington, on November 5.

1917

Russia The Czar is forced to abdicate amid mounting popular protest at the war and the worsening food situation. A provisional government is established but Lenin returns from exile demanding power for workers' councils or Soviets and an end to the war. Kerensky becomes prime minister and declares Russia a republic. The Bolsheviks stage a successful insurrection in the capital, St. Petersburg, and take power demanding "Peace, land, bread and all power to the Soviets."

Middle East British and Indian troops capture Baghdad and Gaza from the Turks.

United States declares war on Germany on April 6 — among opponents is U.S. Congress's only female member, Jeanette Rankin. U.S. troops head for France.

France French, British and Canadian soldiers rebel against the inhuman conditions in the trenches. Hundreds are shot by their own officers.

Britain Married women over 30 win the vote.

United States Suffragists picketing White House arrested during August and November.

1918

Russia withdraws from World War I, accepting Germany's peace terms, surrendering Poland and Lithuania and acknowledging the independence of Ukraine. Civil war between the Red Army and the anti-Bolshevik Whites begins. The Czar and his family are executed. Britain and the United States send forces to help the counterrevolutionary Whites.

Syria Arab forces led by Emir Feisal and T. E. Lawrence (Lawrence of Arabia) take Damascus from the Turks.

Germany surrenders on November 11. The Kaiser abdicates and flees as revolution takes hold. Seven other German kings, princes and dukes are chased out of their castles. The Spartacists of Karl Liebknecht and Rosa Luxemburg declare a free socialist republic but social democrat Friedrich Ebert assumes control and clamps down on revolutionaries.

World The death toll from World War I exceeds 10 million.

"Help!" poster from the Russian Revolution, 1921

1919

Germany The Spartacist revolutionaries organize mass rallies and seize public buildings, but the revolt is suppressed. Rosa Luxemburg and Karl Liebknecht are murdered by right-wing paramilitaries. Soldiers' and workers' councils declare Bavaria a socialist republic but troops from Berlin put down the revolution.

Russia The Communist International or Comintern is established.

Hungary Communist uprising led by Bela Kun is quashed by counterrevolutionary forces and Romanian troops within 133 days.

Italy Benito Mussolini founds the Fasci di Combattimento or Fascist Party.

Mexico Rebel leader Emiliano Zapata is killed by government troops.

World The League of Nations is established, to be based in Geneva, but President Wilson cannot persuade U.S. Congress to join. The Versailles Peace Conference imposes humiliating terms on Germany. British Prime Minister Lloyd George predicts another war in 25 years "at three times the cost."

North America Major strikes break out in Winnipeg, Boston and Seattle as returning soldiers confront new labor conditions. A six day general strike is held in Seattle.

India British troops open fire on a peaceful demonstration in Amritzar, killing 379 and wounding 1,200. The shooting follows Mohandas Gandhi's call for a "hartal" or business strike protesting the new security laws.

United States Communist Party founded on September 1.

Ireland Sinn Fein forms a provisional Irish Parliament, or Dail Eireann, with Eamon De Valera as president. Britain sends troops to disband it.

Britain A U.S.-born viscountess, Nancy Astor, becomes the first woman to sit in parliament. The first woman elected to the British parliament was a Sinn Fein member for Dublin in 1918, but she refused to take her seat.

United States Legionnaires attack IWWs in Centralia, Washington, on November 11.

1920

United States Women win the vote. 2,700 radicals are arrested in a swoop on "reds" by the attorney general; membership of a communist party is ruled sufficient grounds for deportation.

Germany Machine guns are turned on the crowd as a peaceful left-wing demonstration turns into an assault on the Reichstag (parliament). The National Socialist German Workers' Party is launched with Adolph Hitler as its spokesperson.

Russia Trotsky's Red Army is victorious against the Whites.

United States Marcus Garvey's Universal Negro Improvement Association holds its first national convention in Harlem on August 1. Socialist Eugene V. Debs receives 900,000 votes in presidential election whilst in prison.

Palestine The League of Nations awards Britain the mandate to rule Palestine.

Ireland The Irish Republican Army (IRA) is formed. Britain deploys ruthless special constables, the "Black and Tans." Hunger striker Michael Fitzgerald dies after 68 days' fast, soon followed by Thomas MacSwiney, Mayor of Cork. The IRA kills 14 British officers in their beds; 300 police barracks are attacked. Martial law is declared.

World The International Feminist Congress is held in Geneva.

India The Indian National Congress adopts Gandhi's program for nonviolent noncooperation with British rule.

Lebanon is created by France.

Britain Sylvia Pankhurst is jailed for six months for calling on workers to loot the docks.

1921

Ireland Britain sends in tanks to Dublin. Sinn Fein wins 124 of 128 southern Irish seats; Ulster Unionists win 40 of 52 northern Irish seats. De Valera agrees to a ceasefire so that talks can begin. At negotiations in London, IRA leader Michael Collins signs a treaty agreeing to the partition of Ireland.

Russia Trotsky crushes an insurrection by sailors in Kronstadt. Lenin introduces the New Economic Policy in an attempt to kick-start the economy but it is too late to stave off mass famine.

Rwanda is ceded to Britain by Belgium.

Germany Hitler becomes leader of the National Socialists.

China Sun Yatsen is elected president but civil war breaks out again between the north and south. A Communist Party is launched in Shanghai.

United States Bill Haywood jumps bail to Russia in March.

United States Italian anarchists Sacco and Vanzetti are framed and convicted of murder.

Mongolia declares its independence from China as the world's second communist state.

Morocco Spain's 2,000-strong garrison at Melilla is wiped out by Berber rebels under Abdel Krim, who declares an independent republic in the hills, inspiring Muslim nationalists all over North Africa.

United States The racist Ku Klux Klan takes over a university in Georgia, saying it will teach "Americanism."

India Gandhi sets light to a huge bonfire of foreign cloth and clothing during the visit of the heir to the British throne.

Italy Mussolini's Fascists, funded by business, win 35 parliamentary seats; his blackshirts regularly beat up socialists and break strikes.

"Never doubt that a small group of thoughtful, committed citizens can change the world. Indeed, it's the only thing that ever has."

–Margaret Mead

1922

Ireland The Dail narrowly approves the treaty setting up the Irish Free State but De Valera rejects it. Civil war breaks out as the anti-treaty IRA fights the troops of the new government and its former leader Michael Collins, who is shot dead in Cork.

India Congress suspends its civil disobedience campaign due to excessive repression. Gandhi is sentenced to six years in prison for sedition.

Egypt is granted independence by Britain and King Fuad becomes sultan. Nationalists object: Britain retains control of defense and the Suez Canal. King Fuad claims Sudan.

Russia Lenin repudiates all debts incurred under the Czar but is incapacitated by a stroke. Russia renames its empire the Union of Soviet Socialist Republics.

Italy Workers at Fiat's car factory in Turin strike against U.S. production-line techniques but the army is called in. Mussolini's Fascists capture the cities of Fiume and Bologna by military force.

They break up a communist-led strike in Milan and seize control of the city. 24,000 blackshirts march unopposed into Rome and King Victor Emmanuel agrees to Mussolini becoming dictator.

United States At least 57 African Americans are lynched by racist mobs in the course of the year as Ku Klux Klan-inspired violence mounts.

1923

Germany Riding the wave of national resentment against war reparations, Hitler attempts a putsch, calling for a march on Berlin; he is imprisoned.

Italy Mussolini rounds up hundreds of socialists and dissolves all opposition parties.

United States Two Louisiana judges and 30 New York police are revealed to be members of the Ku Klux Klan. The Klan refuses to release its membership list but claims to be a million strong.

India Congress resumes civil disobedience.

Mexico Pancho Villa is murdered.

Southern Rhodesia Britain agrees to an autonomous (but white-only) government.

Turkey becomes a republic with Mustafa Kemal as its first president.

1924

Soviet Union Lenin dies on January 21. A council of Zinoviev, Kamenev and Stalin succeeds him, excluding Leon Trotsky.

Britain elects its first Labour Government with Ramsay MacDonald as prime minister. A second election results in a conservative landslide after right-wingers forge a letter to Labour leaders from the Russian leader Zinoviev.

Italy Mussolini's Fascists win a huge electoral majority; socialist Giacomo Matteotti denounces their intimidation and fraud — and is murdered by a gang of fascists 10 days later.

Brazil 250 die as rebels take Sao Paulo.

India Hindus and Muslims clash; Gandhi begins a 21-day hunger strike as "a penance and a prayer."

United States J. Edgar Hoover appointed FBI director.

1925

Soviet Union Trotsky is ousted from the Communist Party leadership by Stalin and put under house arrest. His key supporters are arrested or exiled.

Chile The military overthrows the government in a coup d'état.

United States The Ku Klux Klan parades in Washington on August 8.

Turkey Kurds rebel against Kemal's government.

China Sun Yatsen dies. Chiang Kaishek succeeds him as leader of the southern nationalist party, the Kuomintang. U.S. troops are deployed throughout the civil war.

Germany Hitler publishes *Mein Kampf* (My Struggle).

Morocco Abdel Krim's rebels take on the French colonial forces.

South Africa Nonwhites are barred from skilled and semi-skilled jobs by a new law. Afrikaans becomes the official language.

1926

United States Year-long Passaic textile strike begins in January.

Persia Former cavalry officer and Prime Minister Reza Khan Pahlevi crowns himself shah.

Britain A general strike begins in support of coalminers protesting at wage cuts. It lasts only nine days, but the miners fight on alone for six months. 100,000 women march for peace.

Morocco Abdel Krim's rebellion is crushed by a huge Franco-Spanish force. He is exiled to Reunion Island.

Dutch East Indies Nationalists in Java rebel against Dutch rule.

1927

China Having captured Hankow, Chiang Kaishek's Kuomintang forces take Shanghai; 600 alleged communists are executed.

Dutch East Indies Ahmed Sukarno founds the Indonesian Nation.

Bolivia 80,000 indigenous people stage a revolt against the government.

Nicaragua Rebels under Augusto Sandino attack government troops at Las Flores.

Soviet Union Trotsky and Zinoviev are expelled from the Communist Party.

1928

Nicaragua Sandino's rebels clash with U.S. Marines, killing five. The United States sends 1,000 more marines. The rebels capture U.S.-owned mines.

Britain gives the vote to all women over 21.

China Chiang Kaishek's forces finally take Beijing and he becomes president. He invites U.S. car magnate Henry Ford to become an economic adviser.

1929

Italy's Mussolini claims a 99 percent vote in an election with no opposition.

Soviet Union Trotsky is exiled and 1,600 of his followers are sent to Siberia. France, Germany and Britain refuse him asylum.

India Nehru calls for rebellion if India does not achieve autonomy soon. Gandhi is elected president of the Congress Party but refuses to accept the post.

Germany Communists fight police in Berlin for three days.

World The Geneva Convention is signed by 48 countries, regulating the treatment of prisoners of war.

United States The Wall Street stock exchange crashes, and the world tumbles into economic depression. In October more than three million people are unemployed.

1930

Spain The dictator General Primo de Rivera resigns. Republicans stage an abortive coup.

Brazil The military seize power, ousting a presidential clique that has ruled for 40 years.

Ethiopia Haile Selassie, or Ras Tafari, is crowned emperor and king of kings. The only other black head of state in Africa is in Liberia.

India peacefully celebrates a mock-Independence Day. Gandhi marches 500 kilometers from Ahmedabad to the sea to make salt, in protest at the British monopoly on salt production. He is arrested and imprisoned while 2,500 followers are beaten by police.

United States Unemployment reaches 4.5 million.

1931

India Britain agrees to scrap the salt tax in return for an end to civil disobedience. Negotiations with Gandhi falter.

Nicaragua Following a major earthquake in the capital, martial law is declared; Sandino's rebels capture Puerto Cabezas and the United States promises to withdraw its marines.

Spain Republicans win a landslide victory in elections; King

Alfonso abdicates. Alcara Zamora becomes president.

China In Shanghai, the British arrest the leader of the Indochinese Communist Party, Ho Chi Minh.

United States Striking miners fight armed thugs in Harlan County, Kentucky.

United States Eight million people are now unemployed.

1932

India The Congress resumes civil disobedience; Gandhi and Vallabhai Patel are arrested. Gandhi begins a hunger strike in support of voting rights for "Untouchables;" they are granted.

United States Strikers killed by cops at Ford's Dearborn, Michigan, plant on March 7.

Germany Hitler loses the presidential election to Hindenburg but gains 37 percent of the vote. The Nazis become the largest party in the general election.

Portugal Antonio de Oliveira Salazar becomes fascist leader.

United States Unemployment tops 13 million. President Franklin D. Roosevelt promises a "New Deal" to combat the Depression with public spending. Troops used against World War I vet protest.

Britain Unemployed workers stage hunger marches from the north. There are pitched battles with police.

1933

Philippines The U.S. Congress votes to offer independence in 10 years, despite veto attempt by President Hoover.

Spain Anarchists, anarcho-syndicalists and communists stage a revolt in three provinces and aim to disrupt railway and telephone services; there is a general strike. Communists attempt to seize power following right-wing electoral gains.

Germany Hindenburg appoints Hitler as chancellor of Germany after weeks of street battles between Nazis and communists threaten civil war; within a month the Reichstag is burned down. Freedom of speech and assembly are suspended. The Nazis arrest 65,000 leftists and open the first concentration camp at Dachau; Hitler orders a boycott of Jewish business; Jews start to flee into exile. Hitler bans trade unions and opposition parties and burns books by "un-German" authors. Mixed Aryan-Jewish marriages are forbidden and people with disabilities are to be sterilized. Germany quits the League of Nations.

Britain 30,000 Jews demonstrate against the German Nazis; Oswald

Mosley's fascists start peddling anti-Semitic propaganda.
Cuba Mass protest against President Machado's dictatorship
leads to a coup led by Sergeant Fulgencio Batista.
India Gandhi fasts to the point of death in protest at being
refused the right to work with "Untouchables" while in prison.

"First they came for the communists, and I did
not speak out because I was not a communist.
Then they came for the socialists, and I did not
speak out because I was not a socialist.
Then they came for the trade unionists, and I
did not speak out because I was not a
trade unionist.
Then they came for the Jews, and I did not
speak out because I was not a Jew.
Then they came for me, and there was no one
left to speak for me."

–Pastor Martin Niemoller

1934

Nicaragua Rebel leader Augusto César Sandino is invited to the
presidential palace where he is murdered by National Guards
led by General Anastasio Somoza.
United States General strike in San Francisco begins July 16.
Spain Socialist and syndicalist trade unions call a nationwide
strike against the right-wing government. Catalonia's bid for
independence is crushed.
China Led by Mao Zedong, 100,000 communists begin the
Long March from Kiangsi, where they are surrounded by
700,000 Nationalist troops, to Yenan, 10,000 kilometers north.

1935

Africa A wave of strikes breaks out against colonial labor condi-
tions, starting in the Central African copper belt.
Libya is created by merging the three Italian colonies of
Cyrenaica, Tripoli and Fezzan.
Eritrea and **Somalia** merge to become Italian East Africa.
Ethiopia Italy invades. The League of Nations imposes sanctions.
Bolivia and **Paraguay** finally end the three-year Chaco War over

disputed territory, which has cost 100,000 lives.

China Japanese troops march into Beijing and set up a puppet state in the north. Mao's communists reach the end of their arduous one-year Long March; 70,000 out of 100,000 died en route.

1936

India Nehru becomes Congress leader in the wake of the party's national electoral success.

Spain The left comes to power under Premier Manuel Azana and 30,000 political prisoners are freed. General Francisco Franco leads a right-wing rebellion using foreign legionnaires from Spanish Morocco and is backed by Italy and Germany. Spain is split in half by a bitter civil war as the Republican government moves from Madrid to Barcelona. "La Pasionaria" declares, "They shall not pass!" in response to the fascist rebellion.

Paraguay The military seizes power and establishes the first fascist regime in the Americas.

France Following sit-down strikes by 300,000 workers, the Socialist Popular Front wins the election and grants workers a 12 percent pay rise, a 40-hour working week and two weeks' paid holiday.

Britain Unemployed people begin the Jarrow March to London. 100,000 people build barricades to stop Mosley's fascists marching through London's East End.

1937

Spain Britain and the United States ban their citizens from fighting in Spain under threat of imprisonment, but about 59,000 men and women flock from all over the world to join the International Brigade to aid the Republican antifascist cause. Franco's Nationalists have just as large a foreign contingent, mostly Italian and German soldiers. Hitler bombs the Basque city of Guernica.

United States General Motors recognizes United Auto Workers (UAW) on February 11 after Flint sit-down strike. On May 26 company cops beat up UAW leaders at River Rouge, Michigan.

China The Japanese attack Beijing and Shanghai. Chiang Kaishek reluctantly concludes a military alliance with Mao Zedong's communists.

United States Police kill ten strikers at Republic Steel on May 31.

1938

Spain Franco starts bombing the Republican capital, Barcelona. His troops win a series of crushing victories in Catalonia.

United States House Un-American Activities Committee formed on May 26.

China Japan bombs Canton into submission.

Czechoslovakia Britain and France agree to hand over Czechoslovakia to Germany. British leader Neville Chamberlain praises Mussolini's Italy and declares he has negotiated "Peace for our time."

Germany On *Kristallnacht,* November 9, Nazis embark on anti-Semitic violence, hundreds of synagogues are torched and thousands of shops looted.

1939

Spain Fall of Spanish Republic on March 28. Franco's fascist forces take Barcelona and Madrid, winning the Civil War.

Japan Fascist Baron Hiranuma takes over as prime minister.

United States Supreme Court declares sit-down strikes illegal in judgment on February 27.

Soviet Union Stalin signs a Nonaggression Pact with Hitler on August 23.

Poland is invaded by Germany on September 1. Mass deportations of Jews begin.

World France and Britain declare war on Germany on September 3. The United States, the Soviet Union, Sweden, Norway and Belgium declare their neutrality.

United States Albert Einstein warns President Roosevelt of the danger of the atomic bomb.

1940

Palestine Britain authorizes the transfer of land from Arabs to Jews.

Poland Nazi Heinrich Himmler constructs the Auschwitz concentration camp.

United States Anticommunist Smith Act passed on June 28.

United States 937 Jewish refugees on *SS St. Louis* turned away in New York harbor.

Mexico The exiled Leon Trotsky is murdered by one of Stalin's agents.

1941

Ethiopia Haile Selassie's troops recapture Burye from the Italians. South African troops capture Addis Ababa and Haile Selassie reenters after five years' exile.

United States Ford recognizes UAW on June 20.

France Fascist leader Marshal Petain arrests 12,000 Jews.

Indochina Japanese troops take over Cambodia, Thailand and Vietnam. Ho Chi Minh launches the Vietminh independence movement.

Japan bombs the U.S. fleet in Pearl Harbor, Hawaii, then invades Hong Kong, Malaya and the Philippines.

United States enters the war. The American Federation of Labor (AFL) pledges no strikes in war plants.

"Nationalism is an infantile sickness. It is the measles of the human race."
–Albert Einstein

1942

Japan attacks the Solomon Islands and New Guinea. It captures Singapore, Java, Burma and the Philippines.

United States The Supreme Court outlaws Georgia contract labor as peonage in a judgment on January 12.

Germany The Nazis agree on "The Final Solution," the systematic extermination in death camps of Europe's 11 million Jewish people. They begin deporting Jews to Auschwitz.

Poland The Warsaw Ghetto, where 350,000 Jews have been confined, is attacked and thousands of its occupants killed or sent to concentration camps.

United States 100,000 Japanese Americans are rounded up, to be held in camps for the duration of the war. U.S. planes bomb Tokyo.

India Congress launches the "Quit India" campaign.

1943

United States Anarchist Carlos Tresca is murdered in New York on January 11.

Soviet Union German forces at Stalingrad surrender on February 2, a major turning point in the war. The Red Army advances, liberating captured cities.

Pacific A major U.S. offensive begins at Guadalcanal in the Solomons.

Poland The remaining Jewish inhabitants of the Warsaw Ghetto fight bravely against death squads but are ultimately massacred.

Italy U.S. troops invade Sicily. Mussolini is deposed and antifascist Marshal Badoglio takes over. Italy surrenders and declares war on Germany. King Victor Emmanuel is dethroned.

World Stalin, Roosevelt and Churchill meet in Tehran on November 28 to discuss the shape of the post-war world.

Yugoslavia Partisan leader Josip Broz Tito sets up a provisional government.

United States Race riots take place in Los Angeles (June 5-8) and Detroit (June 20-22). Army used to put down protests.

1944

India Famine in Bengal kills three million. The British direct grain elsewhere to help the war effort on Churchill's orders.

World The July Bretton Woods conference in New Hampshire plans the financial architecture of the post-war world; it leads to creation of International Monetary Fund (IMF) and the World Bank.

Palestine The Zionist Stern Gang assassinates Britain's Middle East minister in Cairo.

Vietnam The Vietnamese People's Army is formed under Vo Nguyen Giap.

Greece Britain invades. The leftist National Liberation Front tries to seize power but Britain intervenes on the right-wing side.

Guatemala A popular rising, the "October Revolution," overthrows General Castañeda.

United States Wartime profits for 1944 total $10.8 billion ($6.4 billion in 1940). There are more strikes than any previous year in U.S. history.

1945

Poland Red Army liberates Auschwitz on January 26.

Germany Allied bombers reduce Dresden to ruins during February 13-14, killing 130,000 civilians. Allied troops capture Berlin; Hitler and Himmler commit suicide. German troops surrender on May 8. Nazi leaders Goering and Hess go on trial for war crimes at Nuremberg.

Philippines is liberated from Japanese occupation.

poster © OSPAAAL

World At Yalta and Potsdam, Soviet, U.S. and British leaders meet to carve up the post-war world. The war has cost 55 million lives, including 20 million Soviet citizens, 15 million Chinese and six million Jews. The United Nations is established, along with the IMF and the World Bank.

Africa A Pan-African Congress organized by Kwame Nkrumah is held in Manchester, England.

Balkans Watched by the Soviet Union, Bulgaria, Romania and Yugoslavia all have communist victories in elections.

Indochina Cambodia and Vietnam both declare independence.

Italy Mussolini is shot dead by partisans.

Burma The British take Rangoon.

Japan The United States drops atomic bombs on Hiroshima (August 6) and Nagasaki (August 9). Japan surrenders on August 14, although intercepted radio transmissions in July had shown that Japan was already preparing to surrender.

Indonesia Sukarno's Nationalists declare war on the Dutch colonialists; their rebel republic is recognized by the departing Japanese.

Palestine Arabs in Jerusalem begin a general strike and riot in Cairo in protest at Zionism.

Syria and **Lebanon** win independence from France.

1946

World UN General Assembly meets for the first time in London.

Vietnam Ho Chi Minh wins elections in the north. The French bomb Haiphong on November 23.

China Nationalist-communist civil war erupts.

Egypt Britain withdraws all its troops.

Czechoslovakia Communists win elections.

Palestine Both Jews and Arabs are outraged at an Anglo-U.S. plan recommending continued British control. Zionist guerrillas blow up the British Army headquarters in Jerusalem. Britain refuses to allow any more Jewish refugees from Europe to enter and stops ships docking. The United States protests.

Italy votes to abolish its monarchy.

Argentina General Juan Perón becomes president.

India Congress rejects Britain's latest plan for independence. The Muslim League prepares for civil war in pursuit of a separate state of Pakistan. Thousands die in Hindu-Muslim conflict.

Nehru is appointed head of a provisional government.
Algeria Ferhat Abbas proposes an independent republic.
Philippines gains independence on July 4.

1947

India and **Pakistan** win their independence from Britain on August 15. An estimated 8.5 million refugees cross the border in both directions in "the largest migration in history." Around 400,000 die in intercommunal violence. Gandhi fasts for Hindu-Muslim unity. The Maharajah of Kashmir opts to join India rather than Pakistan; Muslim guerrillas resist the decision.
United States Truman calls for a crusade against communism. The Marshall Plan will offer aid to help the recovery of noncommunist Europe. The House Un-American Activities Committee investigations intensify, Hollywood is targeted and blacklisting begins.
Morocco Rebel leader Abdel Krim, who has escaped from Reunion Island after 11 years, demands an end to French rule.
Palestine anti-British Zionist terrorism increases. The number of Jewish immigrants refused entry and held in Cyprus camps reaches 20,000. The UN votes for partition between Jews and Arabs.
Indonesia The Dutch crack down on nationalists.
Burma U Aung San, hero of the independence movement, is assassinated just before Britain agrees to relinquish control of the colony.
Greece The United States sends massive aid to prop up right-wing Greek Government.

1948

India Gandhi is assassinated on January 30. The army compels the Muslim ruler of Hyderabad to accede to India. The war with Pakistan over Kashmir continues.
Ceylon gains its independence from Britain.
Palestine descends fast into civil war. Eight hours before the British mandate is due to expire, Jews declare the new state of Israel on May 14. It is immediately recognized by the United States.
Korea The Soviet-backed North under Kim Il Sung and the U.S.-backed South under Syngman Rhee each claim jurisdiction over all Korea.
South Africa Afrikaner Nationalists win the election and institutionalize the apartheid system.

Philippines Huk peasant rebellion begins. U.S. military intervenes using the Philippines as a counterinsurgency laboratory.
Malaya Communist rebels are brutally repressed by the British Army.
China Communist forces capture Manchuria.
Cambodia gains independence from France.
Indonesia Dutch troops arrest key independence leaders and control all of Java.
World The UN adopts the Declaration of Human Rights.

1949

China Mao Zedong's communist forces triumph over Chiang Kaishek's Nationalists. Mao proclaims the People's Republic of China. Nationalists take refuge on the island of Taiwan.
Indonesia The Dutch withdraw after UN demands. Sukarno becomes president of the Republic of Indonesia after 20 years of struggle.
Israel's first election results in a Labour Government. A truce is signed with Egypt and Transjordan, which is soon renamed Jordan.
Europe The Western powers form the North Atlantic Treaty Organization (NATO) on April 4.
Laos gains its independence from France.
Soviet Union explodes its first atomic bomb.
Greece Left-wing rebellion crushed.
United States 11 communists sentenced under the Smith Act.
World Pope Pius XII excommunicates all communists.

1950

United States Alger Hiss found guilty on January 25 of perjury. Senator McCarthy claims there are 205 communists in government. During the year, Hollywood blacklistees are imprisoned.
Vietnam Ho Chi Minh's Hanoi-based regime is recognized by the Soviet Union and China. France, Britain and the United States back Bao Dai's Saigon-based regime. Ho's Vietminh continue their battle against the French colonial army, pushing it out of the border zone with China.
China and the Soviet Union conclude a formal alliance. China is denied its seat at the UN.
Australia Prime Minister Menzies bans the Communist Party and seizes its assets.

Jordan annexes the West Bank, which had been seen as a Palestinian homeland.

South Africa Black protest at the government's apartheid policies increases. A day of mourning is held in Cape Town against racist legislation.

Korea The North invades the South on June 25 and captures the capital, Seoul. The UN Security Council calls for member nations to help the South resist the invasion. The United States sends troops on June 29; Britain and Australia soon follow. U.S. forces retake Seoul and invade the North on October 7, soon capturing the capital Pyongyang. Chinese troops enter Korea on November 26 to push them back again.

Tibet China invades and takes control.

"When I give food to the poor, they call me a saint. When I ask why the poor have no food, they call me a communist."

–Dom Helder Camara

1951

Korea Chinese and U.S. forces cross and recross the border between North and South at the 38th Parallel. General MacArthur wants to attack China but is fired by President Truman. A truce holds most of the year during peace talks.

South Africa removes the vote from people of mixed race.

Iran nationalizes the British-run oil industry.

Egypt rescinds its alliance with Britain. Anti-British riots erupt. Britain offers a defence pact but is rejected. British troops seize the Canal zone. Egyptian guerrillas fight back with police help.

United States The Supreme Court upholds the Smith Act on June 4.

1952

Egypt 17 Britons are murdered in Cairo riots. General Muhammad Neguib and Colonel Gamal Abdel Nasser seize power, later proclaiming a republic.

Cuba General Fulgencio Batista carries out a coup on March 10.

Gold Coast Kwame Nkrumah wins the British colony's first election

while in prison for sedition, becoming the first African Prime
Minister.
Vietnam France launches a huge offensive against the Vietminh.
South Africa The ANC mounts a defiance campaign against
racist laws.
Kenya The anticolonial battle is joined as Africans take the Mau
Mau oath to drive out whites. The European colonial elite
forms a Home Guard. Britain sends troops. The leader of the
Kenya African Union, Jomo Kenyatta, is arrested as 2,500 Mau
Mau suspects are rounded up.
Eritrea becomes part of Ethiopia as British troops finally leave.
United States explodes first Hydrogen bomb on November 1.

1953

Kenya The Mau Mau uprising mushrooms; the governor impos-
es the death penalty for taking the Mau Mau oath; 1,000 Kikuyu
are rounded up near Nairobi; Jomo Kenyatta and five col-
leagues are given seven years' hard labor; 99 are killed in a
British attack on rebel strongholds.
Soviet Union Stalin dies on March 5.
Laos The capital Pakseng falls to Ho's Vietminh.
Korea War ends after two million have died.
Australia Britain explodes two nuclear bombs in the South
Australian desert, land inhabited by Aborigines.
Cuba Fidel Castro leads an assault on Batista's military barracks
in Santiago de Cuba; the July 26 assault fails, many are killed
and others are imprisoned, including Castro.
Morocco The French depose the sultan.
Iran A CIA-backed coup ousts nationalist Prime Minister
Mossadegh on August 19.
British Guiana The left-wing People's Progressive Party rebels
against colonialism; Britain sends troops, suspending the consti-
tution.
Jordan Israeli troops attack three villages, killing 56 people.

1954

Kenya Mau Mau leaders, Generals China, Katanga and
Tanganyika, are captured. The British try and fail to engineer a
mass surrender, instead they round up 65,000 Africans for ques-
tioning.
British Guiana People's Progressive Party leader Cheddi Jagan is

jailed for six months.

British Honduras The anti-British People's United Party wins the election.

Egypt Nasser becomes leader after a power struggle, forcing Britain to withdraw troops from Suez within two years. He cracks down on the fundamentalist Muslim Brotherhood after it tries to assassinate him.

Vietnam Vo Nguyen Giap's Vietminh forces capture the French stronghold of Dien Bien Phu on May 7 after a 55-day siege, humiliating the colonial power. The French are forced to sue for peace and back the partition of Vietnam into North and South. The Vietminh take Hanoi.

Guatemala The elected government of President Jacobo Arbenz, which had been pursuing land reform by expropriating unused land owned by the U.S. United Fruit Company, is deposed on June 29 by a CIA-backed invasion.

United States The Supreme Court rules that racially segregated schools are illegal; southern whites refuse to comply.

Argentina Juan Perón is reelected; he immediately arrests opposition leaders for "disrespect."

Algeria Nationalists led by Ahmed Ben Bella begin armed resistance to French rule.

1955

Third World The first international conference of independent Asian and African countries takes place in Bandung, Indonesia, calling for neutrality of developing countries in the Cold War.

South Africa Police destroy the black township of Sophiatown, bulldozing the homes of 60,000 people in a newly designated white residential area. The ANC holds a "Congress of the People" in Kliptown and adopts a Freedom Charter. The ANC is banned from calling strikes or holding public meetings.

United States Young African American Emmett Till is lynched in Mississippi on August 28.

Vietnam Civil war breaks out between rival factions in Saigon. Emperor Bao Dai remains in his Cannes villa while Premier Ngo Dinh Diem cracks down. Diem declares South Vietnam a republic with himself as president.

World Prominent scientists sign a declaration urging nations to renounce war; they include Albert Einstein and Bertrand Russell.

poster © OSPAAL

Sudan wins independence from Britain/Egypt.

United States African Americans boycott segregated buses in Alabama, inspired by Rosa Parks' refusal to move from a whites-only seat.

"I knew someone had to take the first step and I made up my mind not to move."
–Rosa Parks

1956

Guinea/Angola Amílcar Cabral founds the African Party for the Independence of Guinea and Cape Verde and (with Agostinho Neto) the Popular Movement for the Liberation of Angola (MPLA).

Tunisia is granted full independence by France; nationalist leader Habib Bourguiba becomes president.

Soviet Union Khrushchev reveals Stalin's crimes in speech on February 14.

United States Martin Luther King Jnr. is convicted of organizing the bus boycott in Alabama; he vows to continue the fight for civil rights with "passive resistance and the weapon of love."

Yemen Anti-British strikes in Aden lead to clashes between British and Yemeni troops.

Egypt British troops leave the Suez Canal zone on time but Nasser then takes over the Canal, nationalizing the Anglo-French company that runs it. He rejects a plan for international control of the Canal. On October 31, France, Britain and Israel invade Egypt.

Nicaragua The dictator Anastasio Somoza is shot dead in Panama; his son Luis takes over.

Hungary launches a revolt against Soviet rule. Rebels free Cardinal Mindszenty after eight years in prison. The Soviet Union sends in tanks and a new hardline leader, Janos Kadar, is imposed. About 100,000 refugees pour into Austria.

Poland Thousands demonstrate in Warsaw against Soviet domination, inspired by Hungary.

Cuba Fidel Castro lands on the coast to lead a guerrilla movement against the dictator Batista.

1957

Egypt nationalizes all British and French banks.
Yemen Troops from Yemen invade the British colony in Aden but are driven out.
Israel The UN demands Israeli withdrawal from the Gaza Strip and Aqaba; eventually it complies.
Ghana (formerly Gold Coast) becomes independent; Kwame Nkrumah rejoices that they have shed "the chains of imperialism."
Oman British troops suppress an uprising against the sultan.
Malaya gains its independence from Britain after 170 years; Abdul Rahman is its first premier.
United States Eisenhower sends Federal troops to enforce desegregation in Little Rock, Arkansas.
Haiti François Duvalier (Papa Doc) wins the election.
Australia The seventh British nuclear bomb is exploded at Maralinga; hundreds of Aborigines have died as a result of the tests.
Indonesia Sukarno expels all Dutch nationals in protest at Dutch rule in West Papua.

1958

Venezuela A coup removes dictator Marcos Pérez Jiménez.
Egypt and **Syria** unite to form the United Arab Republic, with Nasser as president.
Britain The Campaign for Nuclear Disarmament (CND) is launched.
Algeria explodes as 40,000 French settlers or *pieds noirs* seize government buildings to support French rule.
France is thrown into crisis by events in Algeria. A referendum grants General de Gaulle absolute power as president. De Gaulle offers all African colonies either independence, or autonomy within the French Union; all but one opt for the latter.
Guinea declares its complete independence from France, led by Sekou Toure.
Haiti Papa Doc Duvalier crushes an attempted coup and will now rule by decree.
Burma General Ne Win takes over in a coup.
Africa The All-Africa Peoples Conference is held in Ghana, inspiring the anticolonial movement across the continent.

1959

Cuba Fidel Castro's rebels topple the dictator Batista, promoting radical land and economic reform. Che Guevara becomes head of the Cuban national bank.

India Nehru's daughter Indira Gandhi is elected president of the Congress Party.

China Mao Zedong launches the Great Leap Forward, accelerating industrialization and rural collectivization.

Southern Africa Anti-British riots break out in Nyasaland and Southern Rhodesia. Britain flies in troops and dissolves African nationalist parties, arresting Hastings Banda and other leaders.

Tibet Rebellion is brutally suppressed; the Dalai Lama flees into exile in India.

Cyprus A peace deal establishes a republic with a Greek President and a Turkish Vice-President. Makarios returns home to become president.

Laos The Pathet Lao communist rebels launch a major offensive.

Algeria De Gaulle offers a referendum, but only after a four-year ceasefire.

Belgian Congo Nationalist Patrice Lumumba is arrested for inspiring an antiwhite riot.

Ceylon Socialist Prime Minister Solomon Bandaranaike is assassinated.

> "We should cease to talk about vague… and unreal objectives such as human rights, the raising of living standards, and democratization. The day is not far off when we are going to have to deal in straight power concepts. The less we are then hampered by idealistic slogans, the better."
> –George Kennan, U.S. State Department, 1948

1960

South Africa The new Progressive Party calls for an end to apartheid. On the first day of a civil disobedience campaign against laws requiring blacks to carry a pass, police open fire on a crowd at Sharpeville township, leaving 56 dead. All black political organizations are outlawed. A state of emergency is declared as

APARTHEID

DIA MUNDIAL DE SOLIDARIDAD
CON EL PUEBLO DE AFRICA DEL SUR   26 DE JUNIO

WORLD DAY OF SOLIDARITY
WITH THE PEOPLE OF SOUTH AFRICA   JUNE 26

JOURNEE MONDIALE DE SOLIDARITE
AVEC LE PEUPLE DE L' AFRIQUE DU SUD   26 JUIN

٢٦ حزيران : يوم التضامن الدولي مع شعب إفريقيا الجنوبية

poster © OSPAAAL

30,000 Africans demand the release of all political prisoners.
Africa French Congo, Chad, Central African Republic, Togo
and Madagascar all gain their independence from France.
Somalia The British and former Italian Somaliland join to form
a new independent state.
Nigeria gains independence from Britain as Africa's most popu-
lous state.
United States 1,000 African American students protest peacefully against segregation in Alabama; a sit-in at a lunch counter is
held in Greensboro, North Carolina, by four African American
students; the Student Nonviolent Coordinating Committee
(SNCC) is formed.
South Korea President Synghman Rhee resigns after a week of
street protest by students at his rigged election victory.
Congo Patrice Lumumba's rebellion wins independence from
Belgium. But copper-rich Katanga province tries to secede, led
by Moise Tshombe. UN troops replace Belgians. Lumumba
declares martial law then invades Katanga. Colonel Joseph
Mobutu seizes power with U.S. and Belgian support; Lumumba
is arrested.
Ceylon Sirimavo Bandaranaike becomes the world's first woman
prime minister.

1961

South Africa Nelson Mandela forms *Umkhonto we Sizwe* (Spear of
the Nation) as the armed wing of the ANC.
Algeria In a referendum on home rule, 15 million French and
Algerians vote "yes" and five million "no." Rebel French Army offi-
cers seize Algiers. A nationwide strike in France supports De
Gaulle. The rebellion falls apart.
Congo Patrice Lumumba is murdered while in custody. UN
forces crush the Katangan rebels. UN Secretary General Dag
Hammarskjold dies in a plane crash while flying to meet
Tshombe.
Angola A nationalist uprising leads the UN to urge Portugal to
reform.
Cuba is invaded by a CIA-run expedition at the Bay of Pigs on
April 17; the invasion is defeated. Meanwhile, the revolutionary
government proceeds with a national literacy campaign.
United States SNCC and CORE Freedom Rides during May.

Kenya Jomo Kenyatta is released after nine years in British custody.

Tanganyika gains independence from Britain with Julius Nyerere as president.

Vietnam Kennedy increases the number of military "advisers" from 800 to 3,000.

Latin America Kennedy launches the Alliance for Progress at Punta del Este to counter Cuba's growing influence.

World First summit of the Nonaligned Nations Movement is held in Belgrade.

1962

Algeria The terrorist group of white settlers and ex-officers extends its bombing campaign to Paris and murders dozens of Muslims in Algiers, trying to provoke full-scale war. De Gaulle orders an all-out assault on the French rebels. OAS leader Raoul Salan is captured and imprisoned. A referendum votes almost unanimously for immediate independence.

Rwanda and **Burundi** become independent of UN trusteeship.

Peru President Prado is deposed in a right-wing coup.

Indonesia The Dutch hand over control of West Papua to Indonesia.

Uganda becomes independent of Britain. So does **Trinidad** and **Tobago**.

United States Whites students at Mississippi University riot after admission of black student James Meredith. Martin Luther King Jnr. and Ralph Abernathy are imprisoned three times in the year for antisegregation protests.

Cuba Missile Crisis and confrontation between the United States and the Soviet Union reaches its climax in October.

South Africa ANC leader Nelson Mandela is jailed.

Mozambique The Front for the Liberation of Mozambique (Frelimo) is launched in Tanganyika.

1963

Peru 800 communists are arrested by the junta.

Southern Rhodesia Black nationalist Joshua Nkomo is sentenced to six months' hard labor.

Africa Leaders from 30 African countries form the Organization of African Unity.

South Vietnam Buddhist monk Quang Duc burns himself to

death in protest at the anti-Buddhist policies of Catholic President
Diem. Diem is killed in a military coup.

United States Martin Luther King Jnr. addresses 200,000 demonstrators in Washington for black civil rights saying "I have a
dream..." A few weeks later racists bomb an African American
church in Birmingham, Alabama, killing four girls attending
Sunday school.

Malaysia comes into being as a federation including Singapore
and part of Borneo; martial law is declared after days of riots.

United States President Kennedy assassinated in Dallas on
November 22.

Kenya gains its independence from Britain under Jomo Kenyatta.

1964

World Developing countries band together at the UN Conference
on Trade and Development (UNCTAD) to form an organization
that will defend their interests; this becomes the Group of 77.

Tanzania is formed when nationalists in the newly independent
island of Zanzibar overthrow the sultan then opt to unite with
Tanganyika.

Brazil A U.S.-backed military coup topples the three-year-old left-
wing government. Paulo Freire, who uses literacy programs to
"conscientize" the poor, is imprisoned, then exiled.

Cyprus descends into civil war between Turks and Greeks. UN
peacekeeping troops arrive.

Palestine Palestine Liberation Organization (PLO) is formed in May.

United States Civil rights activists Goodman, Schwerner and
Chaney are murdered in Mississippi; their bodies are exhumed on
August 4. In the same month, Democrats refuse to seat Mississippi
Freedom Democratic Party delegates at convention.

South Africa Nelson Mandela and Walter Sisulu are given life
imprisonment for treason and sent to Robben Island.

Malawi and **Zambia** gain their independence from Britain. They
were formerly called Nyasaland and Northern Rhodesia and are
led by Hastings Banda and Kenneth Kaunda respectively.

United States Martin Luther King Jnr. wins Nobel Peace prize on
October 14.

Vietnam U.S. troops are committed to war against the North. The
Tonkin Gulf resolution — the legal instrument for escalating U.S.
military intervention in Vietnam — was pushed through Congress

by the Johnson Administration after an supposed attack by
North Vietnamese torpedo boats on U.S. warships.
World Second summit of Nonaligned Nations Movement in
Cairo elects Nasser as chair.

"Our deepest fear is not that we are inadequate. Our deepest fear is that we are powerful beyond measure. It is our light, not our darkness that most frightens us…"
–Nelson Mandela

1965

Mozambique Frelimo leader, Eduardo Mondlane, is assassinated
by Portuguese colonial agents. The liberation movement now
controls a fifth of the territory.
Indonesia Army Chief General Suharto seizes power under the
pretext of stemming "communist penetration." More than one
million leftists and community activists are murdered and
200,000 other activists imprisoned.
Gambia gains independence from Britain.
United States Malcolm X assassinated on February 21. Martin
Luther King Jnr. calls for an end to war in Vietnam.
Vietnam U.S. bombers hit North Vietnam during February; the
first U.S. combat troops in Vietnam arrive on March 8; by mid-
year the number of U.S. soldiers in Vietnam has increased to
125,000.
United States State troopers attack civil rights marchers near
Selma on March 6.
Dominican Republic U.S. Marines invade on April 28.
Algeria Colonel Houari Boumedienne seizes power from
President Ben Bella.
United States Riot against police brutality in Watts, Los Angeles,
in August.
India and **Pakistan** go to war again over Kashmir; Pakistan
bombs Delhi and Bombay while Indian troops attack West
Pakistan.
Rhodesia makes a unilateral declaration of independence from
Britain in order to retain white power. Britain imposes economic
sanctions.
Congo Army Chief General Mobutu seizes power again.

1966

Central African Republic Colonel Jean Bedel Bokassa seizes power.
Ghana CIA assists the overthrow of Kwame Nkrumah.
United States National Organization for Women (NOW) founded in June.
United States Race riots erupt in Chicago, New York and Cleveland.
Botswana (formerly Bechuanaland) gains independence from Britain.

1967

Greece U.S.-backed "Colonels' Coup" on April 21 ousts civilian government.
United States Muhammad Ali stripped of boxing title on April 30 for refusing military draft.
China explodes its first Hydrogen bomb.
Israel wins a crushing victory in the Six Day War against the Arabs, seizing the Sinai peninsula and the Gaza Strip from Egypt; the West Bank and Jerusalem from Jordan.
United States Anti-Vietnam War rally surrounds the Pentagon on October 21. Founding of Youth International Party (Yippies) on December 31.
Bolivia Che Guevara is captured by CIA and U.S.-trained Bolivian Rangers on October 8 and executed the next day.
South Yemen A new republic is formed as Britain pulls its troops out of Aden after 128 years.
Australia After a referendum, Aboriginal people win full citizenship, though not land rights.
Vietnam U.S. planes bomb the North again and use napalm in the South.

"You'll get freedom by letting your enemy know you'll do anything to get your freedom... it's the only way you'll get it."
–Malcolm X

United States FBI launches COINTELPRO (a covert intelligence operation) against black, antiwar and left groups.

1968

Czechoslovakia Liberal Alexander Dubcek comes to power, talking about giving socialism a "human face." He relaxes censorship, arrests the head of the secret police. Soviet tanks crush the Prague Spring experiment on August 20 but thousands of Czechs continue to protest.

Vietnam The Vietcong launch the Tet Offensive, capturing Hue and attacking all over the South. U.S. domestic confidence in the war effort is shattered and antiwar protests erupt all over the world. At My Lai U.S. soldiers rape and massacre innocent villagers. Peace talks start in Paris.

United States Martin Luther King Jnr. is assassinated in Memphis on April 4, sparking urban uprising all over the United States. Thirty nine people are killed.

Mauritius becomes independent of Britain.

France In May, 30,000 students take to the streets of Paris setting up barricades and chanting revolutionary slogans and workers strike in solidarity with the students. De Gaulle cracks down and wins a landslide victory in June elections.

United States Police riot at Democratic Party convention in August.

United States Women's liberation movement organizes a demonstration at Miss America pageant in Atlantic City.

1969

Palestine Yasser Arafat becomes leader of the PLO.

Northern Ireland In May Britain introduces troops in response to rioting.

United States People's Park protest in Berkeley in May.

Vietnam Ho Chi Minh dies.

Libya A coup led by Moammar Qadaffi ousts King ldris and nationalizes foreign banks.

United States Police harassment of gays in New York's Greenwich Village results in gays fighting back; the resultant Stonewall riots become a worldwide symbol of the struggle for gay rights.

Cambodia Nixon and Secretary of State Kissinger start secret bombing, followed by a U.S. invasion.

SOLIDARIDAD MUNDIAL CON LA LUCHA DEL PUEBLO DE PUERTO RICO
WORLD SOLIDARITY WITH THE STRUGGLE OF THE PEOPLE OF PUERTO RICO
SOLIDARITÉ MONDIALE AVEC LA LUTTE DU PEUPLE DE PORTO RICO

poster © OSPAAAL

United States Vietnam Moratorium Day, more than 250,000 rally against the war on November 15.
United States Native American activists seize Alcatraz prison on November 20.

United States On February 18, the black rights activists known as the "Chicago 7" are found not guilty of inciting riot.
Laos U.S. planes intensively bomb the Ho Chi Minh trail, the Vietcong supply line through Laos.
Cambodia Prince Sihanouk is overthrown by right-wing leaders; President Nixon sends U.S. forces into Cambodia in April.
United States The largest student strike in U.S. history takes place in May; four Kent State University students demonstrating against the Vietnam War are shot dead by National Guards in Ohio on May 4. On May 14, police kill two students at Jackson State University.
United States The five-year strike of Hispanic grape pickers in California, and the boycott of Californian wines by 17 million people leads at last to the recognition of the United Farm Workers of America, led by César Chávez.
United States New York legalizes abortion on July 1; women march for the Equal Rights Amendment on August 26.
Tonga becomes independent of Britain.
Northern Ireland Conflict between British troops and the IRA mushrooms. Soldiers use rubber bullets.
Chile Socialist Salvador Allende is elected president despite the CIA's efforts to undermine him and provoke a right-wing coup.
Fiji gains its independence from Britain.
Canada The Quebec Liberation Front kidnaps and murders Provincial Minister Pierre Laporte. Trudeau outlaws the Front, invoking emergency powers.
Syria General Hafez al-Assad seizes power.

Switzerland Women finally win the vote.
Laos South Vietnamese troops invade Laos.
United States Supreme Court upholds busing to desegregate schools in judgment on April 20.
Bangladesh declares its independence from Pakistan; troops from West Pakistan respond shelling civilian areas of Dacca.

Thousands die and almost two million refugees flee into India.
United States On September 13, 1,500 troopers storm Attica
prison, killing 43 prisoners.
India and **Pakistan** go to war, Indian troops invade East Pakistan
and help Bengali fighters establish the new state of Bangladesh.
Vietnam Nixon vows to pull out U.S. troops. The "Pentagon
Papers" — documents detailing secret history of U.S. involvement
in Vietnam — are leaked by Daniel Ellsberg to *New York Times.*
Haiti Papa Doc dies and is replaced as dictator by his son Jean-
Claude Duvalier, or "Baby Doc."
Bahrain gains its independence from Britain.
Uruguay The left-wing Tupamaros release the British Ambassador
who has been hostage for eight months.
United States Environmentalists sail a fishing boat to Amchitka
Island off Alaska, forcing the U.S. to call off a nuclear test; the
direct-action group Greenpeace is born.
China finally takes its seat at the UN, until now held by Chiang
Kaishek's Taiwan.
Chile President Allende's Popular Unity Government nationalizes
the copper mines and undertakes land reform.

"I didn't fight to get women out from behind the vacuum cleaner to get them on to the board of Hoover."
–Germaine Greer

Northern Ireland On Bloody Sunday British paratroops shoot and
kill 13 nationalist marchers for civil rights in Derry. The IRA retali-
ates by bombing the Paratroop headquarters in Britain, killing
seven civilians. Britain imposes direct rule; 100,000 Unionists
protest. The IRA splits over negotiations.
Vietnam Communist troops invade the South. On December 17
the United States launches a massive bombing campaign against
Hanoi and Haiphong in the North.
United States Arrests at Watergate Hotel break-in on June 17. In
October the *Washington Post* exposes Nixon's role in the Watergate
burglary.
United States Supreme Court holds death penalty unconstitutional

1972

in June 29 judgment.

Canada Workers in Quebec strike against repressive labor laws, occupying radio stations.

Nicaragua The capital Managua is destroyed by a massive earthquake; 10,000 die. The dictator Somoza pockets much of the relief aid.

1973

Vietnam Hanoi signs a peace agreement with the United States in Paris; U.S. combat troops withdraw from Vietnam, though military advisers remain.

United States On February 28, the American Indian Movement (AIM) occupies the historic site of Wounded Knee (where 300 Lakota Indians were massacred in 1890) for 71 days, demanding that the U.S. Government honor treaties with Native Americans. Two people are killed.

Lebanon plunges into civil war between the Christian Phalange and Palestinian guerrillas.

Cambodia U.S. planes continue to bomb despite the Paris accord.

Chile A U.S.-backed military coup on September 11 — led by General Augusto Pinochet — overthrows President Allende, who is killed in a two-hour siege of the presidential palace. Massive repression follows as thousands of leftists are rounded up, tortured and murdered, while others flee into exile.

Mozambique The Portuguese colonial army massacres civilians.

Egypt and **Syria** launch a joint attack on **Israel** on the Jewish holy day of Yom Kippur, October 6. Israel recaptures the Golan Heights from Syria but only wins the war after a massive tank battle with Egypt in the Sinai Desert.

Britain Strikes by miners, rail and power workers plunge the country into crisis; a three day working week is imposed.

United States *Roe v Wade* decision by Supreme Court establishes women's rights to terminate pregnancy.

1974

Ethiopia A general strike begins against Emperor Haile Selassie's rule; he is later ousted by a military coup.

Portugal Radical elements in the military bring down Caetano's right-wing regime on April 25.

India tests a nuclear bomb in May.

Greece Seven years of military rule comes to an end.

United states Engulfed by the Watergate scandal, President Nixon resigns on August 9. President Ford pardons him on September 8.

Mozambique Frelimo takes power in a provisional government, led by Samora Machel.

United States Antibusing riots occur in South Boston on September 12 against school desegregation.

1975

Vietnam North Vietnamese forces take Saigon on April 30, reuniting the country at last. Seven million tons of bombs have been dropped during the war, more than twice the number dropped in Europe and Asia during World War II. CIA's "Operation Phoenix" executed over 20,000 civilians as suspected communists.

Cambodia The Khmer Rouge take Phnom Penh; under Pol Pot, the inhabitants of the capital are forced into the countryside, intellectuals are murdered and the country is sealed off from the outside world.

Portugal Left-wing officers defeat a right-wing coup attempt and organize the first free election for 50 years, won by the socialists.

Lebanon The civil war between Christian and Palestinian militias spirals.

Angola gains independence from Portugal but descends into civil war. The MPLA government is challenged by UNITA, which is backed by South Africa. Cuba sends troops to repel apartheid forces. CIA supports Jonas Savimbi's UNITA.

Papua New Guinea wins independence from Australia.

Morocco claims the Spanish Sahara. King Hassan organizes the "Green March" of 350,000 volunteers join troops crossing the border. Half the local Saharawi population is forced to flee into the desert.

Spain Fascist General Franco dies. King Juan Carlos announces a general amnesty.

Australia Labor Government is sacked by the Queen's representative, the governor general, on November 11, prompting a constitutional crisis.

East Timor Indonesian troops invade in December after Timorese declare their independence from Portugal.

1976

South Africa In June, the black township of Soweto erupts as schoolchildren protest the imposition of the Afrikaans language in schools. Workers organize strikes as rioting spreads to townships all over the country when the protests are violently repressed. Several hundred are killed, young militants are forced into exile and join the armed resistance to the apartheid government.

Western Sahara Spain formally withdraws, leaving Morocco and Mauritania to carve up the territory; Saharawi liberation front Polisario initiates armed struggle for self-determination.

Argentina Isabel Perón, president since the death of her husband, is ousted in a military coup.

United States Supreme Court reinstates death penalty in July 2 judgment. Congress passes Hyde amendment on September 16, banning federal funding for abortions.

China Mao Zedong dies.

"The outstanding lesson [of the Vietnam war] is that we should never let another Vietnam-type situation arise again… We have learned the need for a strong police force and a strong police intelligence organization to assist in identifying early symptoms of an incipient, subversive situation."
–General Maxwell Taylor, CIA

1977

Israel Right-wing former Zionist terrorist Menachem Begin becomes prime minister; he gives the green light to Jewish settlement in the West Bank.

Panama United States and Panama sign treaty on September 7 for return of canal.

Djibouti gains its independence from France.

South Africa Black Consciousness leader Steve Biko is killed in police custody.

Egypt President Sadat visits Israel in search of peace; Syria, Libya, Algeria and South Yemen sever ties with Egypt in protest.

1978

Rhodesia Ian Smith's plan for transition to majority rule is rejected by guerrilla leaders Joshua Nkomo and Robert Mugabe.

Afghanistan A Soviet-backed military coup kills almost all government leaders.

Israel and **Egypt** sign a peace deal; Israel is to return the Sinai peninsula.

Iran Mass demonstrations against the shah lead him to impose martial law. Millions take to the streets, hundreds are killed.

Nicaragua Sandinista guerrillas temporarily seize the National Palace and successfully negotiate the release of political prisoners.

1979

Iran Iranian Revolution in February; the shah flees to the United States; exiled Islamic leader Ayatollah Khomeini returns. The U.S. Embassy is stormed and 100 staff taken hostage.

Cambodia Khmer Rouge defeated and Heng Samrin heads new government. The Vietnamese reveal the full horror of Pol Pot's holocaust, in which one and a half million people died.

Rhodesia Final agreement is reached for majority rule in the new nation of Zimbabwe.

Pakistan General Zia introduces Islamic law. He executes former Prime Minister Zulfikar Ali Bhutto.

St. Lucia gains its independence from Britain.

Uganda Tanzanian troops help to depose dictator Idi Amin.

Grenada Grenadan Revolution takes place led by New Jewel Movement and Maurice Bishop.

Britain Margaret Thatcher's Conservatives win the election.

El Salvador 20,000 mourn those killed when soldiers opened fire on a peaceful demonstration outside the cathedral in the capital, San Salvador.

Nicaragua On July 19 the Sandinistas lead the revolutionary overthrow of U.S.-backed dictator, Anastasio Somoza. The FSLN begins instituting popular measures such as land reform and literacy programs.

St. Vincent becomes independent of Britain.

Afghanistan Soviet troops move in and install a new government.

World Sixth summit of the Nonaligned Nations Movement, which now has 95 members, nominates Fidel Castro as chair.

poster © OSPAAL

1980

Afghanistan Islamic nations deplore the Soviet invasion and pledge support for the *mujahideen* guerrillas.

Zimbabwe Robert Mugabe's ZANU party wins the first free election.

El Salvador Archbishop Oscar Romero is assassinated by right-wing paramilitaries at the San Salvador cathedral on March 24.

Iran A U.S. military mission to rescue the hostages ends in disaster when a helicopter crashes in the desert. The **Iran-Iraq** War begins, following border conflict.

Britain NATO decides to deploy Cruise missiles at Greenham Common.

Poland Shipyard workers in Gdansk strike during August.

1981

United States Ronald Reagan becomes president.

Iran releases the U.S. hostages after 444 days, on January 20.

United States In February, Reagan issues the "White Paper" justifying expanded U.S. intervention in Central America.

Northern Ireland IRA prisoner Bobby Sands goes on hunger strike to demand special status as a prisoner of war. He wins a by-election to become an member of parliament then dies as the Thatcher Government refuses to make concessions.

Belize (formerly British Honduras) gains independence from Britain.

Britain Rioting breaks out in nine cities protesting unemployment, poor housing and racism.

Iran The Khomeini Government executes 149 "leftist militants."

Egypt President Sadat is assassinated by Egyptian soldiers outraged at the peace deal with Israel. Hosni Mubarak takes over, vowing to stick with the peace policy.

Western Europe Hundreds of thousands demonstrate against nuclear weapons.

United States On October 2, Reagan proposes a big increase in defense spending, including B-1 bombers and MX missiles.

Guatemala U.S.-armed Guatemalan Army conducts genocide of Indian population.

1982

Argentina captures the Malvinas (Falkland) Islands from Britain, which sends a naval task force to the South Atlantic to retake the territory. The war gives Prime Minister Thatcher confidence to push forward with extreme right-wing policies, while the military regime in Argentina is weakened.

Lebanon Israel invades and drives the PLO out of Beirut. With Israeli leader Ariel Sharon's O.K., Lebanese Christian militia massacre Palestinian refugees in the camps of Sabra and Chatila. Israel retains control of the southern third of the country.

United States On June 30, the Equal Rights Amendment for women falls three states short of ratification.

Poland Demonstrations continue against martial law and for the trade union Solidarity, which is banned.

Nicaragua Backed by the United States, 2,500 of Somoza's former National Guard (now called *contras*) invade from Honduras to attack the Sandinista revolutionary government.

United States Up to a million people rally in New York's Central Park calling for nuclear disarmament. But the next year President Reagan unveils his "Star Wars" plan for a missile shield to protect the United States from nuclear attack.

"Bombs may kill the hungry, the sick and the ignorant, but bombs cannot kill hunger, disease or ignorance. Nor can bombs kill the righteous rebellion of the peoples."

–Fidel Castro

1983

Europe Protest against the deployment of nuclear Cruise missiles intensifies. At least one million stage the largest demonstration in West Germany since the war. In Britain the women's peace camp is established at Greenham Common.

Chile Nationwide demonstrations call for an end to Pinochet's dictatorship.

Philippines Opposition leader Benigno Aquino is shot dead at the airport as he arrives home from exile to fight an election against the dictator Ferdinand Marcos. Three million attend his funeral.

Grenada In October, Prime Minister Maurice Bishop is arrested and killed by a clique within the New Jewel Movement. On October 25, U.S. Marines invade and depose the government.

Lebanon 241 U.S. Marines and 58 French paratroopers die in

suicide bombings by Shia Muslims. The PLO has to quit Tripoli for
Tunisia.

Argentina ends military rule as Raúl Alfonsín becomes the first
civilian president for eight years.

1984

Uruguay Protests against military rule, including a 24-hour general
strike, force elections and a return to civilian government after 11
years.

Britain Coalminers go on strike; regular confrontations with police
help turn the strike into a watershed battle between the union
movement and the right-wing Thatcher Government. The miners
finally return to work after a year.

Mozambique signs a peace accord with South Africa, which has
supported the brutal, right-wing Renamo rebels.

India A toxic leak on December 3 from the U.S. transnational
Union Carbide's chemical plant at Bhopal kills 2,500 people and
affects 50,000 others in the worst industrial accident in history.

Burkina Faso is the new name for Upper Volta, a year after revolutionary Thomas Sankara has come to power.

Philippines Almost a million take to the streets of Manila on the
anniversary of Aquino's death.

Nicaragua Sandinista leader Daniel Ortega is elected president.

Ethiopia is engulfed by famine, caused by civil war and drought.
The scale and severity touches the world as no African famine has
before. At least half a million die of starvation.

New Zealand The new Labor Government bans nuclear-armed and
nuclear-powered ships from the country's ports.

1985

World The UN Conference on Women takes place in Nairobi,
Kenya, attended by 10,000.

New Zealand The Greenpeace ship *Rainbow Warrior is* blown up in
Auckland harbor by French secret agents before it can lead a
protest at the Mururoa Atoll nuclear-test site.

Western Sahara The Saharawi Arab Democratic Republic is admit-
ted to the Organization of African Unity; Morocco responds by
resigning.

1986

Philippines President Marcos claims an electoral victory but "people power" forces him to back down. Corazon Aquino, widow of the assassinated opposition leader, becomes the new president on February 25.

Haiti Jean-Claude "Baby Doc" Duvalier is overthrown as dictator and flees into exile in France.

Libya The United States bombs Qadaffi's home on April 14 and 15, killing his daughter.

Ukraine Meltdown at Chernobyl nuclear power plant in Ukraine kills thousands and sends toxic clouds across Europe.

South Africa The apartheid regime concedes to grant people of mixed race and Indians the vote and their own chambers in parliament; "Africans" are still excluded. Black resistance turns many township areas into no-go areas for the police. Millions of black people strike for a day on the 10th anniversary of the Soweto Uprising on June 16. A nationwide state of emergency is imposed.

United States Congress passes sanctions against South Africa on October 2 despite Reagan's veto.

Mozambique President Samora Machel is killed in a plane crash in South Africa.

1987

Fiji Colonel Sitiveni Rabuka stages a coup, proposing a racially discriminatory new constitution.

United States Iran-Contra investigation reveals illegal covert actions by Reagan administration to aid *contras* fighting to overthrow Nicaraguan Government. The International Court finds the United States in abrogation of international law for its embargo against Nicaragua, mining its harbors and creating and supporting *contras*.

Burkina Faso Revolutionary leader Thomas Sankara is murdered by colleague Blaise Compaore, who takes over as president.

Palestine An *intifada* explodes among Palestinians in Israeli occupied territories on December 9.

1988

Afghanistan Soviet Union withdraws troops.

Brazil Outspoken activist Chico Mendes, who works with Amazonian rubber tappers and indigenous people, is murdered by landed interests.

poster depicting massacre of Palestinian refugees at Sabra and Chatila
© OSPAAAL

Burundi Thousands die in ethnic conflict between Tutsi and Hutus.

Pakistan General Zia dies when his plane explodes. Benazir Bhutto is elected to replace him — the first female leader of a Muslim country.

Middle East The Iran-Iraq War ends in August after eight years.

Australia Hundreds of thousands of Aborigines and supporters protest 200 years of white invasion and racist policies.

1989

Paraguay General Alfredo Stroessner is overthrown as labor, indigenous and women's protest helps end 35 years of dictatorship.

Iran Ayatollah Khomeini dies.

Alaska The *Exxon Valdez* oil spill in March.

China Students occupy Tiananmen Square in Beijing seeking more democracy.

Poland Solidarity is legalized and partially democratic elections are held.

South Africa President F. W. De Klerk releases eight ANC leaders from jail, including Walter Sisulu.

East Germany Erich Honecker is ousted. The Berlin Wall is pulled down by demonstrators. The communist leadership resigns.

Canada Mohawks occupy ancestral ground that is to be a golf course, becoming a rallying-point for native struggles across North America.

Panama The United States invades Panama on December 20, capturing former ally President Noriega and killing thousands of civilians.

1990

Namibia achieves independence from South Africa. The liberation movement SWAPO forms a government under Sam Nujoma.

South Africa The ban on the ANC is lifted after 30 years. Nelson Mandela is released from prison after 28 years.

Nicaragua After a decade of war, the Sandinista Government loses the election to a U.S.-backed coalition headed by Violeta Chamorro.

Chile General Pinochet resigns the presidency, but remains head of the army. Patricio Aylwin is elected to replace him.

Soviet Union disintegrates as Latvia, Estonia, Uzbekistan, Moldova, Ukraine, Belarus, Armenia all declare independence.

Burma The first multiparty election for 30 years is won by the National League for Democracy. The military rejects the result and arrests Aung San Suu Kyi, daughter of nationalist martyr U Aung San.

Germany is reunited as East Germans vote to join the Federal Republic.

Poland Solidarity's Lech Walesa is president.

Iraq invades **Kuwait** on August 2. The UN Security Council imposes sanctions.

"The most potent weapon in the hands of the oppressor is the mind of the oppressed."

–Steve Biko

Iraq On January 16 the United States bombs Iraq, beginning the Gulf War.

Somalia Rebels take Mogadishu and send President Siad Barre into exile; but civil war breaks out between rival clans and war-lords.

United States Beating of Rodney King by police on March 3 is videotaped. The following year police are cleared and riots break out in Los Angeles, marines are deployed.

Angola A peace agreement seems to end the civil war.

Cambodia A peace treaty ends 12 years of war between the government and the Khmer Rouge.

Haiti Democratically elected President Jean Bertrand Aristide is ousted in a coup.

South Africa Apartheid is legally ended.

Soviet Union is disbanded. Boris Yeltsin becomes Russian president.

1992

Algeria Islamic fundamentalists take up arms after the government cancels elections they are poised to win; they assassinate President Boudiaf; a state of emergency is declared.

Australia The High Court rejects "terra nullius," the idea that the land was empty before British arrival and recognizes indigenous Australians' prior ownership of land and native title.

El Salvador The 12-year civil war comes to an end as the government and the left-wing FMLN guerrillas sign a peace accord. More than 75,000 have died.

Canada A referendum narrowly rejects limited autonomy for Quebec.

Zaire 30 die as the dictator Mobutu's troops fire on a peaceful demonstration led by the clergy.

Peru President Alberto Fujimori suspends the constitution and begins rounding up his critics; police capture Abimael Guzman, leader of the Sendero Luminoso guerrillas.

Afghanistan The *mujahideen* — Muslim resistance fighters — take control of the capital, Kabul; but the civil war between rival factions goes on.

Angola UNITA rebels go on the rampage after they lose the UN-monitored election.

Mozambique President Chissano and Renamo sign a peace treaty. Over a million have died in the civil war.

World The Earth Summit on environmental change in Rio in June is hampered by the negative attitude of the United States. Worldwide protests mark the 500th anniversary of Columbus's arrival in the "New World."

United States On October 23, Congress tightens the economic blockade of Cuba.

Somalia 35,000 U.S. troops land in December.

United States On December 24, President Bush pardons Iran-Contra coconspirators.

1993

Indonesia puts East Timor rebel leader José Xanana Gusmao on trial.

Somalia U.S. troops clash with thousands of protesters in

Mogadishu. In October, Clinton sends more troops to Somalia, after 12 Rangers are killed. The mission is a disaster.

Eritrea wins its independence from Ethiopia after two decades of armed struggle.

1994

Mexico In January, the Zapatista uprising in Chiapas protests the North American Free Trade Agreement (NAFTA) between Mexico, Canada and the United States.

Rwanda Political crisis leads to ethnic clashes in which 500,000 Tutsis are killed and one million Hutu refugees flee.

South Africa The ANC wins 62 percent of the vote in the first free and democratic election. Nelson Mandela becomes president.

Australia/PNG Papua New Guinean villagers successfully sue the transnational BHP for environmental damage caused by the Ok Tedi mine.

Nigeria The military regime imprisons Ogoni leader Ken Saro-Wiwa. Nobel Prize winner Wole Soyinka flees into exile.

Haiti Threatened by U.S. invasion, military leaders cave in and allow President Aristide to return.

Mozambique The Frelimo Government wins the first free elections; Renamo accepts the result.

Namibia President Nujoma and SWAPO win by a landslide in the first post-independence election.

1995

World The World Trade Organization (WTO) comes into being on January 1.

World 5,000 delegates from 181 countries attend the Fourth UN World Conference on Women in Beijing.

Mexico The army sweeps into Chiapas. Over 100,000 demonstrate in Mexico City, demanding the army's withdrawal and peace with the Zapatistas. Later 100,000 march against government austerity measures.

France resumes nuclear testing in Polynesia; riots explode in Tahiti in protest.

Israel/Palestine Israel and the PLO sign an interim agreement allowing limited Palestinian self-rule in the West Bank; Israeli leader Yitzhak Rabin is assassinated by a Jewish right-winger on November 4.

Nigeria The regime executes Ken Saro-Wiwa.

Bosnia A U.S.-brokered deal divides the country into two parts, one for Serbs and the other for Muslims and Croats.

1996

Cuba United States passes the Helms-Burton Law — the harshest-ever economic embargo.

Sierra Leone The first democratically elected government for 20 years signs a ceasefire with rebels after five years' fighting that killed 10,000.

Indonesia Thousands demonstrate against the Suharto regime.

Afghanistan Kabul falls to the extremist Taliban, formerly U.S. allies in anti-Soviet fight. It is decreed illegal for women to work.

Guatemala A peace pact is signed ending a 36-year conflict that killed 140,000.

1997

Zaire/Congo After 32 years in power, Mobutu's corrupt, dictatorial rule is ended by the army of Laurent Kabila, who renames the country the Democratic Republic of the Congo.

China Britain hands over Hong Kong, which it had ruled since the end of the First Opium War in 1842.

Brazil Thousands of landless people march from Sao Paulo to Brasilia demanding land reform.

Western Sahara Polisario and the Moroccan Government sign an agreement aimed at a referendum on the future of the country in 1998.

World The Ottawa Treaty banning antipersonnel landmines is signed after a long campaign.

1998

Sudan United States destroys pharmaceutical plant causing over 30,000 civilian casualties.

Chile Former dictator General Pinochet arrested in London for genocide and terrorism.

Indonesia Suharto regime collapses after 32-year dictatorship.

1999

Yugoslavia United States and NATO forces bomb Yugoslavia during March and June.

East Timor Indonesia is finally forced to withdraw and acknowledge East Timor's vote for independence.

United States Protests at WTO meeting in Seattle in December organized by unions, environmentalists, religious, political and student activists symbolize the growing international opposition to corporate globalization.

Venezuela Hugo Chávez elected president.

2000

Palestine Provocation by Israeli leader Ariel Sharon sparks new *intifada*.

Cuba Fidel Castro at South Summit in Havana, convened by Group of 77, calls for abolition of IMF.

"A world once divided into two armed camps now recognizes one sole and pre-eminent power, the United States of America. And they regard this with no dread. For the world trusts us with power, and the world is right. They trust us to be fair, and restrained. They trust us to be on the side of decency. They trust us to do what's right."

–George Bush Snr., 1992

"Every nation in every region now has a decision to make. Either you are with us or you are with the terrorists."

–George W. Bush, 2001

THREE

ASSASSINATION TARGETS

William Blum

Following is a list of prominent foreign individuals who have been targeted for assassination by the United States since the end of World War II. The list does not include several assassinations in various parts of the world carried out by anti-Castro Cubans employed by the CIA and headquartered in the United States.

1949	Kim Koo, Korean opposition leader
1950s	CIA/Neo-Nazi hit list of numerous political figures in West Germany
1955	José Antonio Remón, president of Panama
1950s	Chou En-lai, prime minister of China, several attempts on his life
1950s	Sukarno, president of Indonesia
1951	Kim Il Sung, premier of North Korea
1957	Gamal Abdul Nasser, president of Egypt
1955	Jawaharlal Nehru, prime minister of India
1958	Brig. Gen. Abdul Karim Kassem, leader of Iraq
1959, 1969-72	Norodom Sihanouk, leader of Cambodia

1950s-1970s	José Figueres, president of Costa Rica, two attempts on his life
1961	Patrice Lumumba, prime minister of the Congo (Zaire)
1961	Gen. Rafael Trujillo, leader of Dominican Republic
1963	Ngo Dinh Diem, president of South Vietnam
1959-late 1990s	Fidel Castro, president of Cuba, more than 600 attempts on his life
1960s	Raúl Castro, head of Cuban Armed Forces
1965-66	Charles de Gaulle, president of France
1965	Pierre Ngendandumwe, prime minister of Burundi
1965	Francisco Caamano, Dominican Republic opposition leader
1967	Che Guevara, Cuban leader
1970-73	Salvador Allende, president of Chile
1970	Gen. René Schneider, commander-in-chief of army, Chile
1970s	General Omar Torrijos, leader of Panama
1972, 1988-89	General Manuel Noriega, chief of Panama Intelligence
1975	Mobutu Sese Seko, president of Zaire
1976-79	Michael Manley, prime minister of Jamaica
1982	Ayatollah Khomeini, leader of Iran
1983	Miguel d'Escoto, foreign minister of Nicaragua
1984	The nine *comandantes* of the Sandinista (FSLN) National Directorate
1985	Sheikh Mohammed Hussein Fadlallah, Lebanese Shiite leader (80 people killed in the attempt)
1981-87	Muammar Qaddafi, leader of Libya
1990-91	Saddam Hussein, leader of Iraq

From William Blum, *Killing Hope: U.S. Military and CIA Interventions since World War 2* (Monroe, Maine: Common Courage Press, 1995)

"Throughout the world, on any given day, a man, woman or child is likely to be displaced, tortured, killed or 'disappeared,' at the hands of governments or armed political groups. More often than not, the United States shares the blame."

–Amnesty International, 1996

RESOURCES

William Blum, *Rogue State: A Guide to the World's Only Superpower* (Common Courage Press, 2000)

Basil Davidson, *Africa in History* (Penguin, 1984)

Eduardo Galeano, *Century of Wind* (London, Minerva, 1990)

Eric Hobsbawm, *Age of Extremes: The Short Twentieth Century 1914-1991* (Michael Joseph, 1994)

Sheila Rowbotham, *Women, Resistance and Revolution* (Penguin, 1974)

Luis Suárez, *Violence and Terror in Latin America* (Ocean Press, forthcoming 2003)

Howard Zinn, *A People's History of the United States. 1492- Present* (Harper Perennial, 1995)

New Internationalist magazine
See also: www.newint.org

www.oceanbooks.com.au/radhist

Chile: The Other September 11

Edited by Pilar Aguilera and Ricardo Fredes

Contributors include: Ariel Dorfman, Salvador Allende, Joan Jara, Beatriz Allende, Pablo Neruda, Victor Jara and Fidel Castro.

For Chileans, the date September 11 has another significance. Following the day in 2001 "when terror descended from the sky" and American hands held up photos of missing loved ones, Chilean author Ariel Dorfman wrote:

"I have been through this before... During the last 28 years, September 11 has been a date of mourning, for me and millions of others, ever since that day in 1973 when Chile lost its democracy in a military coup, that day when death irrevocably entered our lives and changed us forever."

"...when they speak of the bombing of La Moneda Palace in Chile... you should know that this act is the equivalent of bombing the New York Public Library at 42nd Street and Fifth Avenue during the work day."
— José Yglesias September 11, 1974, a year after the coup

radical history

ISBN 1-876175-50-8
80 pages
US$7.95/A$11.95/£5.95
www.oceanbooks.com.au

Politics on Trial
Five Famous Trials of the 20th Century

By William Kunstler

Introduction by Karin Kunstler Goldman, Michael Ratner and
Michael Steven Smith

As the United States once again finds itself adrift in a violent sea of
patriotism, bigotry and fear, it is an appropriate time to address this
country's dark past of political repression and racist scapegoating.

William Kunstler, champion of civil liberties and human rights, reflects
on five famous examples in which ordinary citizens were targeted for
the color of their skin or the views they held. The political trials pre-
sented include those of Sacco and Vanzetti (Italian immigrant anarchists accused of murder); Julius and Ethel Rosenberg (communists
executed for espionage); John Thomas Scopes (convicted of teaching
evolution); and the Scottsboro Nine (nine young African Americans
falsely accused of rape).

About the Author
William Kunstler was the most prominent radical lawyer and outstanding
defender of civil rights in the United States in the second half of the 20th
century. He represented Martin Luther King, Jnr., Marlon Brando, the
Attica prisoners, and the Chicago Seven.

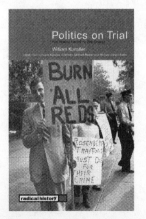

radical history

ISBN 1-876175-49-4
130 pages
US$9.95/A$14.95/£7.95
www.oceanbooks.com.au

rebel lives

"I am in the world to change the world."

Käthe Kollwitz

Ocean Press announces a radically new, radically refreshing series, Rebel Lives. These books focus on individuals — some well-known, others not so famous — who have played significant roles in humanity's ongoing fight for a better world. They are strongly representative of race, class and gender, and they call back from history these lives, catapulting them directly into the forefront of our collective memory.

Rebel Lives presents brief biographies of each person along with short, illustrative selections, depicting the life and times of these

"Better to die on your feet than live on your knees."

Emiliano Zapata

women and men, in their own words. The series does not aim to depict the perfect political model, visionary or martyr, but rather to contemplate the examples of these imperfect theorists, activists, rebels and revolutionaries.

Rebel Lives is produced with assistance from activists and researchers from all over the world, creating books to capture the imaginations of activists and young people everywhere. These books are smaller format, inexpensive, accessible and provocative.

Titles in preparation are:

- Rosa Luxemburg
- Sacco & Vanzetti
- Helen Keller
- Albert Einstein
- "Tania" (Tamara Bunke)
- Chris Hani
- Che Guevara
- Nidia Díaz
- Emiliano Zapata
- Haydée Santamaria

"Philosophers have hitherto interpreted the world. The point now is to change it."

– Karl Marx